Hanna Pahl (Ed.)

Emblematic Strategies in Contemporary Art

Schriften aus dem Kunsthistorischen Institut der Christian-Albrechts-Universität zu Kiel

herausgegeben von

Klaus Gereon Beuckers
Christoph Jobst
und
Uwe Albrecht

Band 7

LIT

Emblematic Strategies in Contemporary Art

Selected Papers from the
Workshop *Emblematic Strategies*
at the University of Kiel,
July 29 – 31, 2014

edited by

Hanna Pahl

with the editorial collaboration of
Justus Gronau

LIT

Cover: Brigitte Kowanz, Just make Sense, 2000, acrylic glass, fluorescent lamps, fluorescent paint, lacquer, 141 × 141 × 19 cm.
Collection Ingrid and Christian Reder, Wien/Vienna.

Photo: Peter Strobl.

This book is printed on acid-free paper.

Bibliographic information published by the Deutsche Nationalbibliothek
The Deutsche Nationalbibliothek lists this publication in the Deutsche Nationalbibliografie; detailed bibliographic data are available in the Internet at http://dnb.d-nb.de.

ISBN 978-3-643-90610-6

A catalogue record for this book is available from the British Library

Klosbachstr. 107
CH-8032 Zürich
Tel. +41 (0) 44-251 75 05
Fax +41 (0) 44-251 75 06
E-Mail: zuerich@lit-verlag.ch
http://www.lit-verlag.ch

LIT VERLAG Dr. W. Hopf
Berlin 2014
Fresnostr. 2
D-48159 Münster
Tel. +49 (0) 2 51-62 03 20
Fax +49 (0) 2 51-23 19 72
E-Mail: lit@lit-verlag.de
http://www.lit-verlag.de

Distribution:
In the UK: Global Book Marketing, e-mail: mo@centralbooks.com
In North America: International Specialized Book Services, e-mail: orders@isbs.com
In Germany: LIT Verlag Fresnostr. 2, D-48159 Münster
Tel. +49 (0) 2 51-620 32 22, Fax +49 (0) 2 51-922 60 99,
E-mail: vertrieb@lit-verlag.de

In Austria: Medienlogistik Pichler-ÖBZ, e-mail: mlo@medien-logistik.at
e-books are available at www.litwebshop.de

Contents

Vorwort

Die mediale Spezifik des Emblems als meist dreiteilige Struktur des textlichen Mottos (*inscriptio*), der bildlichen Umsetzung (*pictura*) und der ausführenden Darstellung (*subscriptio*) besitzt über die im 16. Jahrhundert entstandene und bis in das 18. Jahrhundert blühende Form des klassischen Emblems hinaus eine kunsttheoretische Relevanz. Transmediale Tendenzen, die synoptische Visualität der drei Teile sowie deren inhaltlich changierende Synchroneität sind dabei Aspekte, die auch auf andere kunsthistorische Epochen übertragbar sind und deren Erörterungen auch dort fruchtbar sein können.

Während den Vorbereitungen der 10. Internationalen Konferenz der *,Society of Emblem Studies'*, die vom 27. Juli bis zum 1. August 2014 mit fast zweihundert internationalen Gästen am Kunsthistorischen Institut der Christian-Albrechts-Universität zu Kiel tagte, wurde von den beiden Organisatoren Frau Professorin Dr. Ingrid Höpel und dem Unterzeichner intensiv über visuelle emblematische Strategien und ihre Übertragbarkeit auf zeitgenössische Kunst diskutiert. Den Begriff der ,emblematischen Strategien' hatte Frau Professorin Dr. Mara R. Wade (Illinois) im Sommer 2013 auf einem Kieler Workshop bereits benutzt und er war auch Gegenstand der Diskussion bei der Drucklegung des Kieler Studientages „Architektur als Ort für Embleme" vom Januar 2013. Die beiden Kieler Doktorandinnen Frau Hanna Pahl M.A. und Frau Maren Biederbick M.A. haben die Idee eines Forums, in dem emblematische Strategien an zeitgenössischer Kunst untersucht und an klassischer Emblematik diskutiert werden können, aufgegriffen und als

Nachwuchsworkshop entworfen, durch Mitteleinwerbungen finanziert, organisiert sowie dann vom 29. bis 31. Juli 2014 am Rand der Emblematik-Konferenz mit elf auswärtigen Teilnehmern durchgeführt. Die wechselseitige Konfrontation von klassischer Emblem-Forschung mit aktueller Kunst war sehr erfolgreich und befruchtete die Diskussion über den Workshop hinaus innerhalb der gesamten Konferenz und seitdem weiter im Kunsthistorischen Institut.

Der vorliegende Band versammelt die Beiträge des Workshops zur zeitgenössischen Kunst und ergänzt sie um thematisch passende Beitrage, die im Rahmen der Konferenz vorgetragen wurden. Er wird durch theoretische Überlegungen zu emblematischen Strategien eingeleitet, die Hanna Pahl im Zuge der Vorbereitung erarbeitet und teilweise als Impulse für die Diskussion dort vorgetragen hat. Sie werden jetzt erstmal im Zusammenhang präsentiert und sind in ihrer methodischen und thematischen Gesamtheit ein erheblicher Beitrag für die Emblematik-Forschung.

Im Namen des Kunsthistorischen Instituts der Christian-Albrechts-Universität danke ich Frau Hanna Pahl und Frau Maren Biederbick für die hervorragende Arbeit, die sie für den Workshop geleistet haben. Frau Pahl sei zudem besonders für die Übernahme der Herausgeberschaft dieses Bandes und ihre zügige, gewissenhafte Arbeit gedankt. Dank ihr liegen die Vorträge nun noch nicht einmal ein halbes Jahr nach der Tagung im Druck vor und stehen einer Diskussion zur Verfügung. Dabei wurden die Beiträge weitgehend in Inhalt und Form des Vortrages belassen, um zügig veröffentlicht werden zu können. Die Abfassung in Englisch entspricht der Tagungssprache des Workshops und möchte ausdrücklich Teil einer internationalen Diskussion sein.

Die Realisierung des Bandes wäre ohne die sprachliche Unterstützung von Justus Gronau M.A., der uns als Anglist bei der Redaktion uneigennützig zur Seite stand, so nicht möglich gewesen. Ebenfalls hat unsere Institutsfotografin Kathrin Ulrich einen großen Anteil, die den Band in bewährter Qualität und angenehmer Zusammenarbeit für den Druck gesetzt hat. Beiden sei dafür ganz herzlich gedankt. Ein besonderer Dank gilt zudem selbstverständlich den Autoren, die ihre Beiträge so zuverlässig und kurzfristig zur Verfügung gestellt haben, sowie den Rechteinhabern der Bilder und dem Verlag.

Der Band ist ein relevanter Beitrag zur Erfassung von zeitgenössischer Kunst durch analytische Kriterien und leistet damit in vorbildlicher Weise seinen Teil zu einer der Kernaufgaben kunsthistorischer Beschäftigung mit aktueller Kunst. Das Kunsthistorische Institut freut sich, mit diesem Band ein erstes Paket der Kieler Emblematik-Vorträge von 2014 im Druck vorlegen zu können und hat die Veröffentlichung sehr gerne begleitet. Wir wünschen dem Buch eine große, dem Thema angemessene Resonanz.

PROF. DR. KLAUS GEREON BEUCKERS
Kunsthistorisches Institut der
Christian-Albrechts-Universität zu Kiel

Towards a Theory of Emblematic Strategies in Contemporary Art

Hanna Pahl

This contribution examines and attempts to define characteristics of emblematic strategies in contemporary artworks of the 20th and 21st century.[1] While the presence and the afterlife of emblems in contemporary culture has already been discussed,[2] art historical research has also focused on emblematic *tendencies*, *procedures* and the emblematic *mode* in art and literature of the 20th century.[3] This contribution instead concentrates on the manifold ways in which emblematic *strategies* might reveal new aspects and methodological insights into the contemporary aesthetic practice. The focus on em-

1 The watershed of contemporary art has been defined differently by art historians, philosophers and critics alike. Often, three major periodizations for the beginning of contemporary art are proposed: 1945, the 1960s or 1989. For a discussion of these periodizations see Peter Osborne, *Anywhere or Not at All. Philosophy of Contemporary Art*, London et al. 2013, 18-22. For further information on the concept of contemporary art see, for example, Richard Meyer, *What was Contemporary Art?*, Cambridge, Mass. et al. 2013. – Terry Smith, *What is Contemporary Art?*, Chicago et al. 2009.

2 See Peter M. Daly, "The *Nachleben* of the Emblem in Some Modern Logos, Advertisements, and Propaganda", in: *Companion to Emblem Studies* (AMS Studies in the Emblem, no. 20), ed. Peter M. Daly, New York 2008, 489-517.

3 See *Emblematic Tendencies in the Art and Literature of the Twentieth Century* (Glasgow Emblem Studies, vol. 10), eds. Anthony J. Harper, Ingrid Höpel and Susan Sirc, Glasgow 2005. – Piotr Rypson, "The Emblematic Mode in Twentieth-Century Art", in: *Emblems from Alciato to the Tattoo. Selected Papers of the Leuven International Emblem Conference 18-23 August, 1996* (Imago Figurata Studies, vol. 1c), eds. Peter M. Daly, John Manning and Marc van Vaeck, Turnhout 2001, 335-355. – Daniel Russell, "Icarus in the City: Emblems and Postmodernism", in: *Emblematica* 13 (2003), 333-358.

blematic strategies in contemporary art might also provide new conceptual clarity for the ongoing debate in the field of traditional Emblem Studies, where scholars still discuss the question of what constitutes an emblem in the first place.[4] Here, the aim is not to identify and discuss 'postmodern' emblems,[5] but rather to take a closer look at the processes involved in emblematic strategies.

*

The etymology of the word 'emblem' might serve as an apt starting point for establishing a connection between the Renaissance and Baroque emblems of the 16th and 17th century and positions of contemporary art, which use the concept of arranging and juxtaposing image and text in comparable artistic devices.
Derived from ancient Greek *ἔμβλημα*, one of the etymological meanings of the word emblem is 'mosaic'. As word and image are interdependent in the emblem and it is "technically a composite visual-verbal form"[6], so do the interlocking patterns of the mosaic create new imagery through the combination of different components. In addition to the formal level, the notion of text-image mosaics[7] can also be applied to contemporary art on a semantic level, because the combination of visual and textual, discursive and iconic

4 Conceptual clarity of the term 'emblem' is called for by Rüdiger Zymner, "Das Emblem als offenes Kunstwerk", in: *Polyvalenz und Multifunktionalität der Emblematik. Akten des 5. Internationalen Kongresses der Society for Emblem Studies = Multivalence and Multifunctionality of the Emblem* (Mikrokosmos, vol. 65), eds. Wolfgang Harms and Dietmar Peil, Frankfurt am Main et al. 2002, 9-24.

5 See *Reinventing the Emblem: Contemporary Artists Recreate a Renaissance Idea*, exh. cat. Yale University Art Gallery, ed. Lesley K. Baier, New Haven 1995.

6 W. J. Thomas Mitchell, *Picture Theory. Essays on Verbal and Visual Representation*, Chicago et al. 1994, 215.

7 Julia Kristeva's concept of intertextuality is based on the idea of a mosaic structure: "tout texte se construit comme mosaique de citations, tout texte est absorption et transformation d'un autre texte." Julia Kristeva, "Bakhtine, le mot, le dialog et le roman", in: *Critique* 33 (1967), 438-465, here 440. – The term 'Interpiktorialität' [Interpictoriality] has recently been established within the discussion of image-image quotations or references. See *Interpiktorialität. Theorie und Geschichte der Bild-Bild Bezüge* (Image, vol. 42), ed. Guido Isekenmeier, Bielefeld 2013.

elements leads to processes of codification. In this approach, it is comparable to puzzles or jigsaws[8] not revealing their meaning at first glance. Laurence Grove points out: "For the early reader/viewer the emblem book would have appeared as a sophisticated game, perhaps a jigsaw of which one might see the mosaic as the ancestor."[9] The process of encoding and combining pictorial and textual elements, i.e. different media, can be adapted to the practice of contemporary artists in which the usage of heterogeneous media and the explicit presentation of media changes are constitutive moments. Yet, the emblem book with its bimedial, almost chiastic structure[10] of text and image had already developed a strategy which can be regarded as an early form of intermediality.[11] In analogy to the invention of print culture in the Gutenberg era and the capability of reproducing emblem books, the technical innovations of mass media reproduction of the 20th century enabled artists to broaden the idea of reproduction by creating complex hybrid forms in three-dimensional installations and artworks on the Internet.[12] Using the mosaic-like structure of text-image relations, and enhanced by the medium of sound – for, as John Manning points out, "there are, indeed, musical emblems"[13] – an exemplary Internet-based work by the digital artist

8 See for the picture-puzzle metaphor and the idea of 'pictorial complexity' described by James Elkins as "a certain quality of argument: an attachment to density of thought, and to intricacy" James Elkins, *Why are Our Pictures Puzzles? On the Modern Origins of Pictorial Complexity*, New York et al. 1999, here 11.

9 Laurence Grove, *Text/Image Mosaics in French Culture. Emblems and Comic Strips* (Studies in European Cultural Transition, vol. 32), Aldershot et al. 2005, 125.

10 See Michael Wetzel, *Die Wahrheit nach der Malerei*, Munich 1997, 68.

11 According to W.J.T. Mitchell, "all arts are 'composite' arts (both text and image); all media are mixed media" W. J. Thomas Mitchell, *Picture Theory. Essays on Verbal and Visual Representation*, Chicago et al. 1994, 94-95. – Especially with new media technologies appointed, Marshall Mc Luhan stresses: "The crossings or hybridizations of the media release great new force and energy". Marshall McLuhan, *Understanding Media. The Extension of Man*, 2nd ed., Cambridge, Mass. 1994, 48.

12 Laurence Grove points out that text-image relations in new media art mark a "wider shift towards a three-dimensional text/image culture in what is arguably a new emblematic age." Laurence Grove, "Multi-Media Emblems and their Modern-Day Counterparts", in: Harper et al. 2005 (as note 3), 171-187, here 181.

13 John Manning points out, that "the format of many printed emblems resembles that of the seventeenth-century song books." John Manning, *The Emblem*, London 2002, 20.

Jhave[14] is titled *Mups* (2012).[15] The work's plain appearance is presented as a rectangular window showing 45 horizontally and 28 vertically aligned black squares (1260 in total), which recall the minimalist, geometric sculptures of Carl Andre. In this sense, it alludes to the grid which Rosalind Kraus has proclaimed to be a constitutive concept in modern art.[16] The notion of a text-image mosaic becomes obvious by taking a closer look at the faint gray font above the black squares which provides a linear reading-instruction, also indicated by an arrow pointing from A to Z. This could be conceptualized as the *inscriptio* of the *pictura* challenging the viewer to take an active role in decoding the process. The enigmatic, black squares become emblematic when pointing the cursor over them: in this way, individual *subscriptiones* represented as text information show up for each square. The work is based on an "online sonic mashup engine"[17] containing MP3 files of 1260 audio poems.[18] Clicking on the squares, they immediately turn red and text information of the audio files is presented and listed next to the rectangular window. Thus, a new imagery is created. Simultaneously, the engine can play up to 32 streams of contemporary poems at the same time. Reminiscent of the process of combining the three parts of an emblem into a signifying whole,[19] the synthesis in *Mups* is both realized through the combination of visual and textual parts into a new imagery, and through multilayered sounds of the poetic archive creating a new sound structure.

*

The artistic involvement with digital or analogue media, their citations, appropriations and transformations into new contexts, marks a significant moment in contemporary art recalling the Dadaist and Surrealist practice of collage and photomontage.[20] Benjamin H.D. Buchloh points out in reference to Walter Benjamin's allegory model: "The procedure of montage is one in which all allegorical principles are executed: appropriation and depletion of meaning, fragmentation and dialectical juxtapositions of fragments, and the systematic separation of signifier and signified."[21] Buchloh identifies these simultaneously executed processes within the contemporary artistic practice, in works of Sherrie Levine and Dara Birnbaum, among others. In a similar device, the emblem's *pictura* or the accompanying texts in form of the *inscriptio* or *subscriptio* are often cited, adapted and eventually slightly transformed in different emblem books and for other contexts.[22] Thus, Daniel Russell points out: "The emblem in general is composed of borrowings, fragments, quotations".[23] In addition, there is an obvious analogy between processes of appropriation of text and image and the Situationist theory of *détournement*, which is characterized by the appropriation of "pre-existing aesthetic elements" and the "integration of past or present artistic productions into a superior construction of a milieu."[24] These subversive artistic strategies of appropriation influenced new media artists, especially contemporary software artists[25] and video game artists.[26] Hence,

14 A pseudonym or nickname for Dave Johnston.

15 The title *Mups* is a short form metonymic with *mashups*, which explicitly refers to the technique of collage. For the Jhave's artwork see http://glia.ca/2012/mups/pennsound/ (accessed 1 October 2014).

16 "In the cultist space of modern art, the grid serves not only as emblem but also as myth." Rosalind E. Krauss, *The Originality of the Avant-Garde and Other Modernist Myths*, Cambridge, Mass. et al. 1986, 12.

17 http://glia.ca/2012/mups/ (accessed 1 October 2014).

18 Those audio poems are extracted from the Pennsound archive of the University of Pennsylvania.

19 In this sense, Rüdiger Zymner classifies the emblem as a "synmedial genre". Zymner 2002 (as note 4), 24.

20 For the discussion of works by Max Ernst and René Magritte regarding the comparison between emblematic procedures and compositions see Rypson 2001 (as note 3), 340-341. – John Manning, referring to André Breton, underlines: "Some Surrealist experiments, in which objects were signed and given a new name, have much in common with many emblematic procedures." Manning 2002 (as note 13), 22.

21 Benjamin H. D. Buchloh, "Allegorical Procedures: Appropriation and Montage in Contemporary Art", in: *Artforum*, vol. 21, no. 1 (September 1982), 43-56, here 44.

22 John Manning underlines with reference to the emblem's varying contexts and the adaptation of the *pictura*: "With the advent of amatory and devotional emblematic sub-genres at the beginning of the seventeenth century, a traditional image stock was recirculated within a different context." Manning 2002 (as note 13), 10.

23 Russell 2003 (as note 3), 341.

24 "Definitions", in: *The Situationist International Anthology*, ed. and trans. Ken Knabb, Berkeley 1981, 45-47, here 45.

25 See Florian Cramer and Ulrike Gabriel, "Software Art", in: *DIY Media - Kunst und digitale Medien: Software - Partizipation - Distribution. Transmediale.01*, eds. Andreas Broeckmann and Susanne Jaschko, Berlin 2001, 29-33.

26 See *Gamescenes. Art in the Age of Videogames*, eds. Matteo Bittanti and Domenico Quaranta, Milan 2006.

Corrado Morgana points out: "Détournement is also central to hacker culture; [...] By modding, hacking, exploiting and other strategies of intervention, artists [...] have responded by producing artefacts and activity that re-appropriate dominant culture, where normative tropes and memes are subverted and détourned to produce a counter to expected 'normal' behavior."[27] Apart from the emblems' frequent moral or didactic function, some emblems are indeed "works of social satire".[28] In this case, they might be comparable to certain strategies in contemporary art: Through the artistic act of intervention in new media art, there is a critical or political statement about technological innovations and the unreflecting use of programs and software surrounding the viewer. Recalling our question of what defines emblematic strategies, we can conclude that the proto-acts and processes of quotation, transformation and appropriation in emblems bear a striking similarity to several practices within contemporary art.

*

The 'typical' tripartite structure of the printed emblem consisting of *inscriptio*, *pictura* and *subscriptio*[29] is not entirely transferable to contemporary art in this structural rigidity, because the application of technological innovations generates rather hybrid visual forms.[30] However, there are exceptions, as the emblem often has a "protean structural fluidity"[31] and is not merely a literary phenomenon.[32] In 'Applied Emblematics', the compositional logic

27 Corrado Morgana, "Introduction", in: *Artists Re:thinking Games*, eds. Ruth Catlow, Marc Garrett and Corrado Morgana, Liverpool 2010, 7-14, here 7-8.

28 Manning 2002 (as note 13), 20.

29 See Peter M. Daly, "Emblem Theory: Modern and Early Modern", in: Daly 2008 (as note 2), 43-78, here 46.

30 Ingrid Höpel, however, points out that in the digital work *Things Spoken* of the Hungarian artist Agnes Hegedüs the emblematic tripartite structure of the emblem is indeed formally realized. Ingrid Höpel, "Die Sprache der Dinge. Emblematik und digitale Medienkunst", in: Harper et al. 2005 (as note 3), 151-170, here 156-157.

31 David Graham, "Emblema multiplex: Towards a Typology of Emblematic Forms, Structures and Functions", in: *Emblem Scholarship. Directions and Developments. A Tribute to Gabriel Hornstein* (Imago Figurata, vol. 5), ed. Peter M. Daly, Turnhout 2005, 131-158, here 153.

of the printed emblem does not remain the same. As Peter M. Daly stresses, this is especially the case in the context of architecture: "most architectural emblems have only two parts, *pictura* and *inscriptio*, seldom the third part of the emblem, the *subscriptio*."[33] Furthermore, some emblems lack the pictorial part, a circumstance which John Manning has described as a 'naked' emblem.[34] Keeping these divergent manifestations of the emblem in mind, Dan Graham comes to the conclusion that "an examination of emblematic structure reveals that heterogeneity rather than homogeneity is the rule."[35] On the one hand, this might reveal a structural and conceptual problem, as the identification of emblematic strategies cannot be based on formal levels alone. On the other hand, this heterogeneity of the emblematic structure will enable the comparability with contemporary art if the emblem is conceptualized more like an open form.[36] With regard to the open form, Rüdiger Zymner underlines the emblem's multifunctionality and multivalence on both a semiotic and a semantic level.[37] The partial renouncement of visual or textual components in contemporary art is, for example, either realized through the encoding of textual or algorithmic source code information, through the act of rendering visual elements invisible or in the act of deleting pictorial parts. Contemporary art and emblems share a common aspect; through processes of codification in contemporary art, and the substantial difference of the emblem's several parts or their formal vacancies, these artworks appear highly obscure and enigmatic. In his *Aesthetic Theory*, Theodor W. Adorno has proclaimed the *enigmaticalness* [Rätselcharakter] of artworks as a criterion of all art: "All artworks – and art altogether – are enigmas; since antiquity this has been an irritation to the theory of art. That artworks say

32 See Gerhard F. Strasser and Mara R. Wade, eds., *Die Domänen des Emblems. Außerliterarische Anwendungen der Emblematik* (Wolfenbütteler Arbeiten zur Barockforschung, vol. 39), Wiesbaden 2004.

33 Peter M. Daly, "The Emblem in Material Culture", in: Daly 2008 (as note 2), 411-456, here 413.

34 Manning 2002 (as note 13), 18.

35 Graham 2005 (as note 31), 136.

36 Sabine Mödersheim underlines: "The emblem as an open form allows for variations and adaptations according to differing and fluctuating contexts." Sabine Mödersheim, "The Emblem in the Context of Architecture", in: Daly 2005 (as note 31), 159-175, here 170.

37 See Zymner 2002 (as note 4), 19.

something and in the same breath conceal it expresses this enigmaticalness from the perspective of language."[38]

The processes of codification within different levels of communication are inherent in the work of the Austrian artist Brigitte Kowanz. She uses the medium of light as the central artistic element in her oeuvre.[39] The assumption that language is light is presented in Kowanz's artworks in several ways: one important language system she uses is the Morse code system as one of the first forms of communication at the speed of light. Kowanz's work *Just make Sense* (2000) (fig. cover) is a square acrylic glass with fluorescent paint and laquer, illuminated with fluorescent lamps on the back. The artist shifts the work's title into the picture's center, appearing translated into a linear Morse code consisting of points and dashes. This is a form of language which avoids "ambiguities and vagueness".[40] The linear, geometrical formal aesthetics of the title's phrase is accentuated through positioning the translated words one below the other, thus recalling artistic procedures of concrete and visual poetry.[41] The Morse code system is used as a medium which simultaneously shows and conceals, and therefore is comparable to the Renaissance emblem, in which Reinhard Brandt identifies "a division of work between telling and showing."[42] An emblematic strategy can be identified – even if the message or *sense* of Kowanz's work does not necessarily have to be decoded or translated – as her work highlights the fact that every language

38 Theodor W. Adorno, *Aesthetic Theory*, eds. Gretel Adorno and Rolf Tiedemann, trans. Robert Hullot-Kentor, London et al. 2002, 120 [originally published as: Theodor W. Adorno, *Ästhetische Theorie*, Frankfurt am Main 1970].

39 For the development of light as an independent art form see *Light Art from Artificial Light: Light as a Medium in 20th and 21st Century Art*, exh. cat. ZKM Zentrum für Kunst und Medientechnologie Karlsruhe, ed. Peter Weibel, Ostfildern 2006.

40 Christian Reder, "Licht=Maß=Form=Dasein. Zu Brigitte Kowanz und einem Arbeiten mit Codes", in: *Forschende Denkweisen. Essays zu künstlerischem Arbeiten* (Edition Transfer), ed. Christian Reder, Vienna et al. 2004, 24–34, here 26.

41 See Rainer Fuchs, "Precision without Borders", in: *Brigitte Kowanz. Now I See*, exh. cat. Museum für Kunst und Moderne Stiftung Ludwig Wien/Vienna, ed. Museum für Kunst und Moderne Stiftung Ludwig Wien/Vienna, Nuremberg 2010, 40-46, here 44.

42 Reinhard Brandt, "Sagen und Zeigen / Text und Bild", in: *Die Medien der Künste. Beiträge zur Theorie des Darstellens*, ed. Dieter Mersch, Munich 2003, 93-100, here 95 [translation by author].

or sign system requires learning; this is also the case for many emblems as combining their parts into a signifying whole calls for humanistic learning. Another example of complex processes of encoding the source text in which the viewer is hardly able to decipher the work is implied in a sculpture of the American artist Jim Sanborn, titled *Kryptos* (1989).[43] This public artwork is installed on the grounds of the Central Intelligence Agency in Langley, Virginia. The sculpture resembles the shape of an almost unrolled document consisting of four copper plates with encrypted text in the Latin alphabet. Until now, the work's encoded text has not been deciphered completely. These processes of codification are comparable to the complexity of alchemical emblem books, the hermetic language and "intentionally cryptic symbolism"[44] of which are reserved for the alchemist's inner circle. "[A]nother puzzle for the uninitiated"[45], to draw a line between the alchemist emblem book and contemporary art, is visible in the intentionally intricate work *Kryptos,* in which the code has been invented and developed manually, including explicit aesthetic transformations of the letters in order to complicate the process of decoding.

*

Besides the compositional logic of the emblem, another adequate emblematic strategy in contemporary art is the concept of framing: "The emblem picture is usually framed between motto and epigram."[46] The frame as a visually accentuated formal structure in printed emblems, and certainly subjected to historical developments in its composition, is presented differently: it emphasizes the unity of text and picture or provides a reading instruction by valorizing specific textual or pictorial parts. Furthermore, the frame can

43 See the artist's website for a picture of the work: http://jimsanborn.net/main.html#publicartwork (accessed 2 October 2014).

44 Allison B. Leader, "Historical Emblems: A Provisional Definition of the Genre", in: Exh. cat. New Haven 1999 (as note 5), n. pag.

45 James Elkins, *How to Use Your Eyes,* New York et al. 2000, 106. Elkins refers to the alchemist Stephan Michelspacher and his work *Cabala, Spiegel der Kunst und Natur in Alchymia* (1615).

46 Peter M. Daly, "Emblems: An Introduction", in: Daly 2008 (as note 2), 1-24, here 2.

appear as a text-frame. In contemporary art, the intrinsic relationship between the frame and the framed is enhanced through the institution or discourse which frames. Especially in new media art, the notion of framing shifts by means of the technological possibilities to create new imagery through screens and displays.[47] Lev Manovich additionally points out: "Far from being a transparent window into the data inside a computer, the interface brings with it strong messages of its own."[48] This is realized within another digital work entitled *Untitled Game: Arena* (1998-2001)[49] by the art collective Jodi, formed by the artists Joan Heemskerk and Dirk Peasmans. The work is based on the videogame *Quake I* and its level *Arena*. Jodi erased all graphic elements except for the sound by manipulating the source code

47 This screen-based art has recently been discussed with the term "screen-reliant installation art", where screens take a structuring role in the aesthetic practice. Kate Mondloch, *Screens: Viewing Media Installation Art* (Electronic Mediations, vol. 30), Minneapolis 2010, xii.

48 Lev Manovich, *The Language of New Media*, Cambridge, Mass. 2001, 65.

49 For downloading the emulator of the work see http://www.untitled-game.org (accessed 2 October 2014).

50 In this strategy of the deletion of visual elements, this work is reminiscent of Nam June Paik's work *Zen for Film* (1964), where an unexposed film runs through the projector in an infinite loop.

51 See Uwe Wirth, "Rahmenbrüche, Rahmenwechsel. Nachwort des Herausgebers, welches aus Versehen des Druckers zu einem Vorwort gemacht wurde", in: *Rahmenbrüche, Rahmenwechsel* (Wege der Kulturforschung, vol. 4), ed. Uwe Wirth, Berlin 2013, 15-57.

52 Jacques Derrida, *The Truth in Painting*, trans. Geoff Bennington and Ian McLeod, Chicago et al. 1987, 54 [first published as: *La vérité en peinture*, Paris 1978].

53 John Manning, referring to motifs of play in emblems, underlines with reference to Andrea Alciato: "From the very beginning Alciato identified the composition of emblems with child's play." Manning 2002 (as note 13), 142. – Although not explicitly referring to an aesthetics of play, Piotr Rypson highlights a parallel in the notion of play in emblems and contemporary art: "Nevertheless, something I have called the emblematic mode is present in the arts today, in the continuing play – and struggle – of ideas and images." Rypson 2001(as note 3), 345.

54 Ruth Sonderegger, *Für eine Ästhetik des Spiels. Hermeneutik, Dekonstruktion und der Eigensinn der Kunst*, Frankfurt am Main 2000.

55 Sonderegger 2000 (as note 54).

56 For the 'iconic turn' [ikonische Wendung] see Gottfried Boehm, "Die Wiederkehr der Bilder", in: *Was ist ein Bild*, ed. Gottfried Boehm, Munich 1994, 11-38. – For a similar approach using the term 'pictorial turn' see Mitchell 1994 (as note 6).

57 See, for example, Dieter Mersch, *Ereignis und Aura. Untersuchungen zu einer Ästhetik des Performativen*, Frankfurt am Main 2002. – Martin Seel, *Ästhetik des Erscheinens*, Frankfurt am Main 2003.

in such a way that the moving image – which can be conceptualized as the dynamized *pictura* – is just a plain white screen, although still being framed by the heads-up displays with white font on a black ground.[50] As the work is literally framed by text, it features a form of a title (*inscriptio*) and a subordinated text (*subscriptio*) referring through a white picture to the absent image (*missing sense*). Furthermore, Jodi's *Untitled Game: Arena* is doubly framed because the work is realized through the use of emulation software. The act of double framing in contemporary art leads to the more dynamic concept of a *flexible* frame.[51] In this regard, Jacques Derrida underlines the ambivalence of the frame concept of the *parergon*: "A parergon comes against, beside, and in addition to the *ergon*, the work done [*fait*], the fact [*le fait*], the work, but it does not fall to one side, it touches and cooperates within the operation, from a certain outside."[52]

*

Several emblematic strategies are present in contemporary art. They operate through the mosaic-like motif of combining visual and textual elements, through the processes of citation, appropriation and codification as well as framing. One aspect unites all different levels of emblematic strategies: an aesthetics of play.[53] The emblematic, or rather, hermeneutic circle is set in motion through a process or *interplay* between encoding and decoding, understanding and nonunderstanding. By challenging the viewer in manifold ways, a playful approach to the artwork or the adaptation of ludic motifs can be observed both in emblems and in contemporary art. In Ruth Sonderegger's conception of an *Aesthetics of Play* [Ästhetik des Spiels][54] she highlights that the viewer confronted with an artwork tries to find meaningful relations between the objects or elements. These attempts are marked by an oscillating movement between the formal level and the hermeneutic level of content and meaning. Sonderegger classifies the aesthetic experience grounded in this interplay as an infinite process because dwelling on one pole remains unsatisfactory and points to the other pole, and vice versa.[55] Since the *iconic turn*,[56] contemporary art has discussed and radicalized concepts such as the infinite process of play and questions concerning the aesthetic experience with its phenomenological implications for the nature of perception.[57] Nevertheless, the often playful presentation of the dichotomy of transparency and opacity[58] in contemporary art points to the emblematic strategy of encoding and decoding, which is linked to the interplay of visibility and invisibility. It was the emblem writer Jacob Cats who argued in the beginning of the 17th century: "Experience teaches us that many things gain by not being completely seen, but somewhat veiled and concealed."[59] And it is the contemporary philosopher and art historian Gottfried Boehm who underlines that the "visualization of images is based on absence."[60]

58 See *Hide and Seek. Das Spiel von Transparenz und Opazität*, eds. Markus Rautzenberg and Andreas Wolfsteiner, München et al. 2010.

59 Quoted in: Mario Praz, *Studies in Seventeenth-Century Imagery* (Sussidi Eruditi, vol. 16), Rome 1994, 87.

60 Gottfried Boehm, *Wie Bilder Sinn erzeugen. Die Macht des Zeigens*, 2nd ed., Berlin 2008, 56 [translation by author].

Strategies of Combination and Codification in Contemporary Art Installations

BETTINA DUNKER

Emblematic strategies can be conceptualized as structures which are based on crucial aspects of the emblem like the interaction of picture and text or the enigmatic character of the three-part combination. By extracting emblematic strategies, one can pursue characteristic attributes of the emblem in contemporary art. Peter M. Daly, for instance, detects a 'Nachleben' of emblems in advertisements and logos. He understands modern advertisements as "telling images that communicate symbolically through a mutually supportive combination of text and image that as a mode of rhetoric and a strategy of persuasion is a modern counterpart to the Renaissance emblem."[1] In a similar way, this essay discusses the 'Nachleben' of emblems in contemporary installations. The origin of installation art is mostly placed in the 1960s. By analyzing installations in the context of emblematic strategies, one can gain a new understanding of them. At the same time, it shows the persistence of emblematic ideas long after the heyday of the emblem in the 16th and 17th centuries.

Felix Thürlemann developed his concept of the 'hyperimage' in the face of the text-image structure of the Internet, where everything can be linked together. Still, the 'hyperimage' or 'supra-sign', which Thürlemann understands

1 Peter M. Daly, "The *Nachleben* of the Emblem in Some Modern Logos, Advertisements, and Propaganda", in: *Companion to Emblem Studies*, ed. Peter M. Daly, New York 2008, 489-517, here 491.

as composition of autonomous single works[2], is connected to the emblem. Contemporary installations as well as emblems meet the description of the 'hyperimage' as a sign consisting of several independent units. The emblem is composed of *inscriptio, pictura* and *subscriptio*; together they form one whole. Just as in the 'hyperimage', the combination is not fixed – it can always be changed, creating new emblems that way. Thürlemann suggests: "By integrating it into the wall of pictures, the single painting receives some kind of reading instruction."[3] As I hope to show, the context of the surrounding pictures directs the processes of interpretation – or, in Thürlemann's words, gives a 'reading instruction'.

The method of combination is one crucial emblematic strategy as the emblem combines picture and text to one whole. Daly refers to it in his definition: "'Emblem' can be regarded as a *mode of thought*, which combines pictured thing or word with meaning, and as an *art form* that combines visual image and text."[4] Only the combination of several elements enables the viewer to deduce the meaning of an emblem, because neither part can convey the content without the other. On their own, the *pictura* or the *inscriptio* are often ambivalent – the fact that the same *pictura* or *motto* could be used for different emblems makes this very obvious. The viewer has to combine picture and text to deduce the meaning, while artists use combination to create meanings. It even is possible to produce a new artwork only by other combinations of the same material.

Another constitutive aspect of the emblem is the codification of meaning. Viewed on their own, neither of the emblem parts enables the recipient to understand it completely. And even with all parts put together, the meaning is often still enigmatic, especially when the *subscriptio* is missing. The *subscriptio* contextualizes the topic of the emblem by giving more details, and thereby facilitates the solution to the riddle. This function as a clue to the meaning of the emblem is underlined by examples, which use the respective

2 Felix Thürlemann, "Vom Einzelbild zum Hyperimage. Eine neue Herausforderung für die kunstgeschichtliche Hermeneutik", in: *Les herméneutiques au seuil du XXIème siècle – evolution et débat actuel*, ed. Ada Neschke-Hentschke, Paris 2004, 223-247, here 226.

3 Thürlemann 2004 (as note 2), 234 [translation by the author].

4 Peter M. Daly, "Emblems: An Introduction", in: Daly 2008 (as note 1), 1-24, here 1.

language instead of Latin in the *subscriptio*, whereas the *inscriptio* is still in Latin. It is possible to assume that the national language was employed to facilitate a better understanding of the emblems. In applied emblematics, where emblems are part of architectonical contexts or decorative objects, the *subscriptio* is often missing. Without the *subscriptio*, however, the meaning becomes less clear, and the codification is emphasized. In many respects, contemporary installations are closer to applied emblematics as they also dispense with any text or information towards the interpretation of the work. Instead, the context of the other pictures in the case of the installation, and the architecture and other paintings in the case of applied emblematics, give the 'reading instruction' of the *subscriptio*. In applied emblems and installations the instruction is not expressed in words, so it is more open – and more cryptic at the same time.

Both combination and codification, but especially the latter, have a strong didactic tendency. The mysterious character of the emblem encourages the viewer to look for possible connections between the various parts. The emblem works like a puzzle the viewer is prompted to solve by trying different interpretations. The playful search for the solution requires an active viewer and is also the reason for the didactical value of the emblem. Daly states: "The function of the emblem is didactic in the broadest sense: it was intended to convey knowledge and truth in a brief and compelling form that will persuade the reader and imprint itself on memory."[5] By deciphering the meaning of an emblem, the viewer is thought to learn in a pleasurable way, along the lines of *prodesse et delectare* [to profit and to delight].[6] The viewers are supposed to profit by deducing the emblem's moral quintessence, and at the same time enjoy it by successfully making use of their knowledge and wit. Carsten-Peter Warncke argues that the more wit is necessary on the part of the viewer, the greater the pleasure becomes.[7]

*

5 Daly 2008 (as note 4), 5.

6 This expression has its origin in Horaz' *De arte poetica* and was very popular during the Enlightenment in the 18th century.

7 Carsten-Peter Warncke, *Sprechende Bilder – sichtbare Worte. Das Bildverständnis in der frühen Neuzeit*, Wiesbaden 1987, 171.

How do the emblematic strategies of combination and codification connect with contemporary installation art? It is important to specify the term 'installation', which is so broadly used that it often becomes vague. Installation in the sense applied here does not refer to the mere technical process of objects being 'installed' in an exhibition space. Instead, it is understood as an art form or even medium as Mark Rosenthal argues,[8] comparable to other art media like books, performances or video. As installation art derived from the art practices of the 1960s, there is an obvious interest in site-specificity and the institutional and architectural context as well as time-based art such as happenings and performances.

The installation is characterized by a shift from object-based to context-based art. Michael Archer stresses this shift from object to context and situation in his definition of the installation as "a kind of art making which rejects concentration on one object in favour of a consideration of the relationships between a number of elements or of the interaction between things and their context."[9] In an installation, the meaning does not originate from one or even various objects but from the relationships between these objects and the viewer. Archer states: "Meaning is no longer given, residing in the object until discerned by the perceptive viewer, it is something that is made in the encounter."[10] Similar to that, Julie Reiss defines the installation as "a reciprocal relationship of some kind between the viewer and the work, the work and the space, and the space and the viewer."[11] By involving the viewer in this essential way, the installation is dependent on their participation. Instead of merely passively receiving artworks, the viewer actively puts together the different parts in their mind, and is thereby necessary to complete an installation.

8 Mark Rosenthal, *Understanding Installation Art. From Duchamp to Holzer*, München et al. 2003, 25.

9 Michael Archer, "Introduction", in: *Installation Art*, eds. Nicolas de Oliveira, Nicola Oxley and Michael Petry, London 1994, 8-9, here 8.

10 Michael Archer, "Towards Installation", in: Oliveira et al. 1994 (as note 9), 11-30, here 13.

11 Julie H. Reiss, *From Margin to Center. The Spaces of Installation Art*, Cambridge, Mass. 1999, xiii.

12 Thürlemann 2004 (as note 2), 238 [translation by the author].

Thus, the two essential aspects of the term installation are on the one hand the importance of the context and, on the other the active involvement of the viewer. Importance of context means that in an installation not the objects but the relationships between them are crucial. Accordingly, the key artistic activity for an installation is not creating objects but arranging them. Active involvement of the viewer implies that the participation of the viewer is constitutive for the installation. As most installations are not permanent but created for a specific time and place, the experience of the viewer is the only thing that remains apart from documentation.
This active role of the viewer is also one of the analogies between the installation and the emblem. In the emblem as well as in the installation, the viewer is encouraged to take an active part and look for a meaning of the compilation that exceeds the meaning of the parts regarded separately. Thürlemann underlines: "In the best case, the combination of pictures is also able to call the recipient's attention to a dimension of meaning, which proves to be relevant to the interpretation of one or both works."[12] The enigmatic character of emblem and installation is a playful incentive to find possible meanings of the combination. In this way, for both mediums the involvement of the viewer and their experience is crucial, even if installations have a less obvious didactic character in terms of teaching moral lessons. Another analogy pertains to the multi-part structure of the emblem and the installation. For both, the overall meaning resides in the combination of the parts and the relationships between them. Although emblems usually consist of only two or three parts, while installations can contain hundreds of pictures or objects, the strategies are similar. The relevance of emblematic strategies for installations of Wolfgang Tillmans and Peter Piller is discussed below with the final aim to explore the connection between contemporary installations and emblems.

*

As the number of works marked as installations since the 1990s is huge, it is necessary to find more specific criteria. Thus, the focus lies on installations consisting of several two-dimensional pictures because they provide the possibilities to analyze emblematic strategies without the distraction caused by too heterogeneous materials. In addition, the structure of installations with various pictures and three-part emblems is comparable in terms of that they are both predestined for strategies of combination.

The emblematic strategy of combination is crucial for almost all installations. As the meaning of the installation does not lie in the single pictures, it has to evolve from the relationships between them. This context is built by combination and arrangement of pictures. In recent years, the *Mnemosyne Atlas* (last version 1929) of the art historian Aby Warburg has been interpreted as the first attempt at the current mode of ordering and combining pictures. The *Mnemosyne Atlas* originated from a corpus of 2000 pictures Warburg collected and constantly rearranged on black panels to present them during lectures and in exhibitions. The goal of the *Atlas*, which was not completed because of Warburg's death, was to analyze the reappearance of 'Pathosformeln' of the antiquity – universal formulas that express emotions through gestures and motions – in pictures of the Renaissance and the 20th century. However, this attempt is not to show the impact of antique formulas that made Warburg so popular with current artists and scholars, but his combining of pictures of different character and origin like artworks, stamps, photographs from newspapers and advertisements to create an argument. Georges Didi-Huberman also stresses this aspect: "Above all, Warburg's atlas is a 'tableau' in a combinatorial sense – a 'series of series', as Michel Foucault aptly defined the tableau. This is because he creates an ensemble of pictures, which he then correlates."[13] This strategy of correlation and combination is of great importance for many contemporary installations. In the case of Aby Warburg, who was, after all, an art historian and not an artist, the didactic purpose of creating relationships between pictures is also present. Warburg planned a book with commentary text to go along with the visual tableaus that would have turned the *Mnemosyne Atlas* into a truly emblematic project.

The combination of pictures also characterizes Thürlemann's 'hyperimage', the configuration of which he describes as putting single pictures in a syn-

13 Georges Didi-Huberman, *Das Nachleben der Bilder. Kunstgeschichte und Phantomzeit nach Aby Warburg*, Berlin 2010, 500 [translation by the author].

tagmatic relationship.[14] 'Syntagma' refers to a sequence of linguistic units forming a syntactic unit. What creates the syntagma is the correlation, or combination, of the single units. A contemporary artist known for the constant recombination of his photographs is Wolfgang Tillmans. For every exhibition Tillmans chooses from the total of his accumulated photographs and presents them in a new subjective order. Julie Ault points out: "Tillmans decides on the type and combination of presentation forms according to what seems to be most adequate for a particular work in a certain context and architectonical environment."[15] So, the combination of pictures changes with every exhibition, responding to the context in an architectonical as well as institutional or cultural sense. Because of the always changing combinations, the meaning of the pictures remains in motion. Mary Horlock states: "The connections and networks Tillmans constructs with each collage across a gallery wall summon different narratives and meanings, reflecting his own trains of thought and inviting the viewer to project their own. That the same images exist in multiple formats and contexts ensures there can be no one way of reading them: Tillmans' work is continually changing."[16]
By means of his installation practice, Tillmans avoids to form fixed categories inside his œuvre such as portraits, fashion shots, still lifes or abstract pictures. Neither is there a separation between early and late works, although there are shifts in Tillmans' work: He started with pictures of his social circle in the 1990s, of parties and the gay scene, and only later on began to experiment with various forms of abstract photography. Changing formats support the constant redefinition of his photographs. Tillmans treats every picture equally and constantly puts it in new contexts so that it stays in the process of interpretation. Because of Tillmans' strategy of combination, the pictures are never completed. Tillmans declares in an interview: "Indeed, there is this impulse to finish things – to bring my constant considerations

14 Thürlemann 2004 (as note 2), 226.

15 Julie Ault, "Das Thema lautet Ausstellen. Installation als Möglichkeit in der Praxis von Wolfgang Tillmans", in: *Wolfgang Tillmans. Lighter*, exh. cat. Hamburger Bahnhof Berlin, ed. Joachim Jäger, Ostfildern 2008, 25-33, here 27 [translation by the author].

16 Mary Horlock, "Wolfgang Tillmans", in: *Turner prize 2000. An exhibition of work by the shortlisted artists: Glenn Brown, Michaela Raedecker, Tomoka Takahashi, Wolfgang Tillmans*, exh. cat. Tate Britain London, ed. Mary Horlock, London 2000, n. pag.

and reassessments to a termination. [...] But that is of course incompatible with the creative process. If something is finished, it has no potential any longer."[17] In this sense, the recombination of pictures is crucial for Tillmans' art. It is a possibility to avoid fixed interpretations.

Jan Verwoert describes the effect of Tillmans' installations on the viewer: "Through the complex overall installation technique you are confronted with a moment of visual overload. You have to find ways of orientation in this situation of contiguousness. How do the pictures make meaning? As your eyes move backwards and forwards across the clusters of pictures, you yourself move through the rooms, trying out different viewpoints, searching for clues and connections."[18] The combination of various pictures challenges the viewer to look for the meaning of the arrangement. This is a requirement for installations and emblems alike. Tillmans' way of correlating pictures is also a form of codification, because the meaning of an arrangement can never be completely or finally decoded.

Tillmans underlines that in his installations his decisions are not only about the content, but also about colors, shapes and sizes: "It's an inclusive practice, which allows me to have a little joke in one corner and some sort of personal wink to somebody else in another corner. [...] It's not all personal, although that is one level. The viewer should be encouraged to feel close to their own experience of situations similar to those that I've presented to them in my work."[19] It is impossible for the viewer to piece all layers together, and that is, according to Tillmans, in any case not the aim. Although one can find certain themes in some of the installations, as Tillmans does not announce his underlying considerations, the arrangements cultivate an enigmatic character. That is to say, the installations work with an emblematic strategy of codification because they have a meaning that is not apparent.

17 Wolfgang Tillmans, "Über dieses Buch. Ein Interview von Mary Horlock mit Wolfgang Tillmans", in: *»if one thing matters, everything matters«*, exh. cat. Tate Britain London, ed. Wolfgang Tillmans, Ostfildern 2003, 303-308, here 305 [translation by the author].

18 Jan Verwoert, „Picture Possible Lives: The Work of Wolfgang Tillmans", in: *Wolfgang Tillmans*, eds. Jan Verwoert, Peter Halley and Midori Matsuri, London 2002, 36-89, here 72.

19 Wolfgang Tillmans, "Peter Halley in Conversation with Wolfgang Tillmans", in: Verwoert et al. 2002 (as note 18), 8-33, here 33.

But even if all sources were known, there is no official interpretation one could decipher. Instead, there are countless solutions. Because of this, Tillmans' installations are closer to the more open structure of applied emblematics.

Depending on the juxtaposed pictures, the interpretation for the same picture can differ considerably, in that way demonstrating the possibilities of combination. This can be exemplified by comparing one photograph in different contexts. Tillmans' photograph *Iguazu* represents a detail of the South-American Iguazu Falls, located at the border between Brazil and Argentina. At the top margin of the photograph one can see a few small boats on the water above the edge of the falls. In the center of the picture one sees brownish water rushing downwards and huge white crests. In the bottom corners the picture dissolves into white fog. The picture itself gives no indication of where it was taken; one only sees a detail of a very big waterfall. The title reveals the name and location of the falls, but that does not seem to be the interest of Tillmans' photograph. Rather, it depicts the impressive force of a water fall by focusing exclusively on the water and showing only very little of the surroundings. Tillmans concentrates on the aesthetics of the whirling water that becomes increasingly blurred in the lower half of the picture through the white fog.

In the exhibition 'Neue Welt' [New World] in Zurich, *Iguazu* is part of a linear arrangement (fig. 1). Tillmans combines four large scale photographs on a wall: a still life with an onion (*Onion*, 2010), the interior of a futuristic looking TGV (*TGV*, 2010), an abstract work of the *Silver*-series (*Silver 93*, 2012)[20] and *Iguazu*. On the next wall the line continues with the portrait of an African masai (*Young Masai*, 2012), a detail of a digital star atlas of the European Southern Observatory (*Sensor flaws & dead pexels, ESO*, 2012) and a starry sky (*Paranal ESO, sky & ocean*, 2012). There is no clear link between those pictures, but they all seem to be a part of the 'new world' as Tillmans perceives it. This 'new world' juxtaposes modern technology of trains and astronomical research with things one would not call new, like the tra-

20 The *Silver*-series shows the reaction of photographic paper to light and chemical processes, the title refers to the traces from silver salt stains.

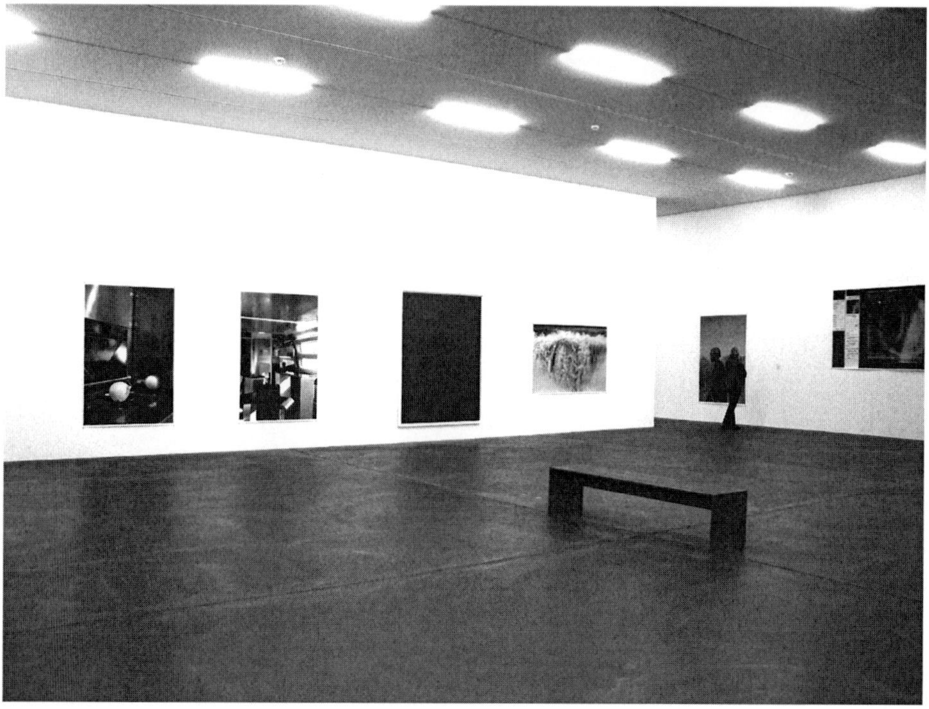

Fig. 1. Wolfgang Tillmans, *Neue Welt,* 2012, inkjet and c-prints (installation view Kunsthalle Zürich). Photo: Bettina Dunker.

ditional lifestyle of the masai or the stars and planets. Still, they form a part of the present world. In this context, the picture of the Iguazu Falls seems to represent one notion of 'nature'. Compared to the planetary system, trains and computers seem very new, and even the monumental Iguazu Falls – underlined through the large scale of the picture – have not always been there. In 2011, Tillmans also uses *Iguazu* for his installation in the Museum of Modern Art in Frankfurt (fig. 2). In this installation, the picture is only 10 to 15 cm. Because of its position next to the right corner of the abstract work *Lighter, blue up VII,* it is reminiscent of a footnote to this work, which consists of a blue, folded paper (fig. 3). In this context, *Iguazu* can be understood as a figurative addition to the abstract blue, a color generally associated with water. Above *Iguazu* there is another very small picture titled *Dürerstraße* [Dürer street], which shows the view through a window into a green garden.

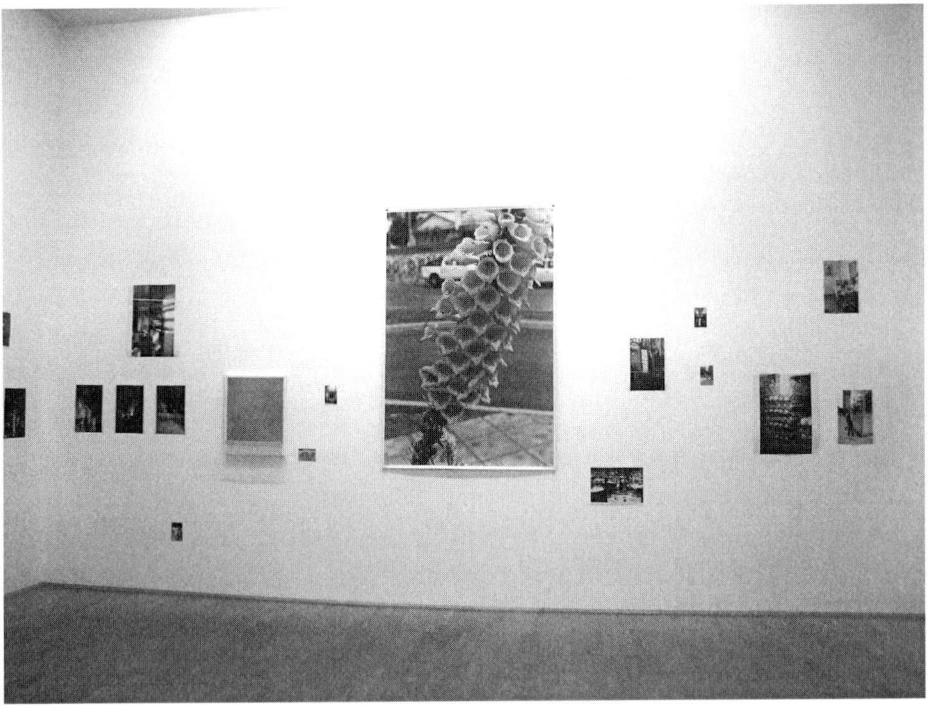

Fig. 2. Wolfgang Tillmans, *Frankfurt Installation 2011*, 2011, 42 inkjet and c-prints (installation view). Museum für Moderne Kunst Frankfurt am Main. Photo: Bettina Dunker.

On the right side of *Iguazu* and *Dürerstraße* hangs a large scale picture of a digitalis (*Ushuaia Digitalis*, 2010). In this neighborhood *Iguazu* seems to deal with beauty that can be found everywhere – whether it is a blooming digitalis next to the street, or a waterfall in the jungle.

As a consequence, the interpretation of *Iguazu* changes, depending on the combination with other pictures, the size and position of it. The photograph itself does not change, but the perception is molded by the surrounding pictures. This example also indicates that although Tillmans installations encourage to look for the reason of the arrangement, there is no clear answer. The interpretation above is just one possibility out of many. It illustrates how combination as an emblematic strategy influences the understanding of a picture, even if the definite meaning remains open. This might reveal one of the fundamental differences between the classical emblem and contemporary art like Tillmans' installations: The aim is not to convey a definite message of a moral kind but to invite the viewers to find their own message. Furthermore, the viewers do not need a humanistic education in order to recognize the symbols and patterns; they only need to employ their personal experience, as Tillmans claims. The content or concept of emblems and installations might be very different, but the strategy of combination, the method to arrange various parts to achieve something new, links them together.

*

It is possible to be under the impression that most contemporary art is codified, as many artworks cannot be understood by just looking at them. The viewer often needs to be aware of an underlying concept to be able to understand the work. The difficulty of understanding contemporary art is even used as a means of intellectual distinction by art collectors, companies, politicians and many more. As Martin Schuster puts it: "The interest in the hard to understand avant-garde is said to mirror the modern and progressive human being able to cope with more sophisticated themes. A certain approach to art, then and now, gives a particular social prestige."[21] Instead of this general mode of codification and its associations of distinction, the focus here is on the involvement of every viewer by presenting a riddle to them. In Peter Piller's installations, codification results from the compilation of various parts. In the case of the emblem, this is a combination of text and picture. Sabine Mödersheim claims there is a tension between text and picture because the link between them is not transparent at first sight – finding it she calls an intellectual game.[22] Most installations do not include text, except a title which can be regarded as a form of *motto*, but there is nonetheless

21 Martin Schuster, *Wodurch Bilder wirken. Psychologie der Kunst*, Köln 1992, 13-14 [translation by the author].

22 Sabine Mödersheim, "Text als Bild: Figurengedicht und Emblematik im Barock", in: *Emblem Studies in Honour of Peter M. Daly*, eds. Michael Bath, Pedro F. Campa and Daniel S. Russell, Baden-Baden 2002, 169-190, here 171.

23 Thürlemann 2004 (as note 2), 238.

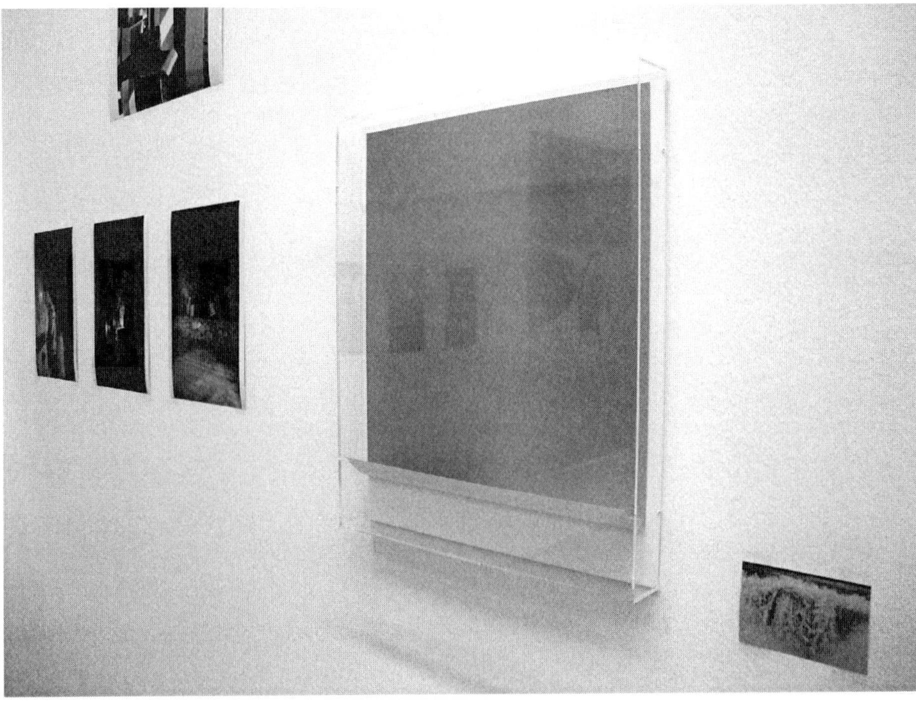

Fig. 3. Wolfgang Tillmans, *Frankfurt Installation 2011*, 2011, 42 inkjet and c-prints (detail). Museum für Moderne Kunst Frankfurt am Main. Photo: Bettina Dunker.

a tension between the pictures because of their enigmatic connections. By putting several images together, the artist suggests there are reasons for the arrangement that can be found by the viewer. Thürlemann describes the search for meaning with regard to the 'hyperimage' as an open process.[23] Without a favored interpretation, the 'hyperimage' allows different understandings, and the viewer is confronted with the task to find their own. Peter Piller's installations operate with this interaction between encoding and decoding.

Piller is especially famous for his archive of approx. 7000 pictures taken from regional German newspapers. He worked in a media agency where he checked the correct placement of advertisements in newspapers and came across his material, which he then organized in surprising and absurd categories like *In Löcher blicken* [looking into holes] or *Eis essende Mädchen* [ice-

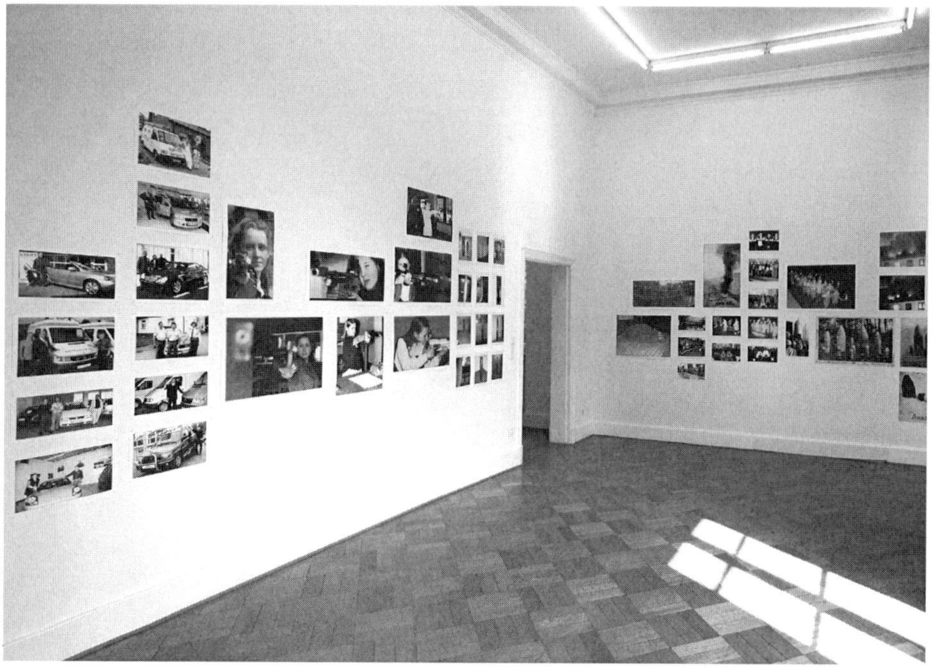

Fig. 4. Peter Piller, *Archiv Peter Piller. Kraft*, 2011, pigment prints (installation view Kunstverein Braunschweig). © Kunstverein Braunschweig / VG Bild-Kunst, Bonn 2014. Photo: Matthias Leitzke.

cream eating girls]. Manisha Jothady calls his working method "recycling",[24] because Piller collects pictures thought to be insignificant and trivial and gives them a new 'life' by including them in his art. The importance of choosing and structuring pictures for Piller's work is stressed by Ludwig Seyfarth: "Initially, there is no idea for Piller, but material that has to be structured and arranged into meaningful relations. [...] In this situation, the artist is inevitably becoming a subjective picture collector and picture selector, whose individuality is less determined by a style or a gesture but in his specific way to open up new relationships between pictures."[25] Piller creates links between pictures and contexts through the accumulation of these pictures. As the reason for the combination is not recognizable at first, it is a form of codification. The artist himself fittingly defines his method of organizing his pictures in the exhibition space as "crossword hanging",[26] which not only refers to the aesthetics of a crossword puzzle, but also to its character as a riddle.

In his artists' books, the subject is known from the beginning because of the title and the original newspaper subtitles are often included. In exhibitions, Piller only presents groups of pictures that have no subtitles. Without text, the codification is enhanced and the pictures are open for more varied information. As the installations only consist of visual information, the focus is on formal and topical analogies, and patterns between the pictures. Recognizing these patterns and reflecting on their meaning is the crucial point of Piller's installations. Friedrich Tietjen describes Piller's archive accordingly: "They are pictures full and very empty at the same time, pictures, in which maybe not much can be discovered in detail, but on the whole, there is much to see."[27]

The analysis of one of Piller's installations clarifies this. Considering one wall of the exhibition 'Archiv Peter Piller. Kraft' at the Kunstverein Braunschweig, one observes a cluster of pictures (fig. 4). Starting from the left side, one homes in on the first group of pictures. They are all the same size, all black-and-white and they all display a car. But there are not only pictures with cars, but also people posing next to or in front of the cars. One pose repeats itself in all pictures, namely, a person leaning towards the car touching it (fig. 5). This almost identically mirrored pose in every shot appears funny, and furthermore suggests that this is a typical motif in regional German newspapers. The seeming frequentness and intimacy between cars and people – Piller calls this group *Auto berühren* [touching car] – leads the viewer to think about the significance attributed to cars in Germany. Piller's pictures remind of car wash every Saturday, small town car sales and the entangle-

24 Manisha Jothady, "Peter Piller. Ein Tennisball, der beim Hecke schneiden zum Vorschein kommt, erinnert an Gewölle", in: *Camera Austria* 89 (2005), 22-30, here 24.

25 Ludwig Seyfarth, "Vorzüge der Absichtslosigkeit. Peter Pillers Archiv verborgener Ikonografien", in: *ars viva 04/05 – Zeit. Michael Hakimi Peter Piller Katja Strunz David Zink Yi*, exh. cat. Kunsthalle Mannheim, ed. Kulturkreis der deutschen Wirtschaft im BDI e.V., Frankfurt am Main 2004, 58-73, here 73 [translation by the author].

26 Jothady 2005 (as note 24), 30.

27 Friedrich Tietjen, "Das Loch im Bild", in: *Fotogeschichte* 104 (2007), 71-73, here 72 [translation by the author].

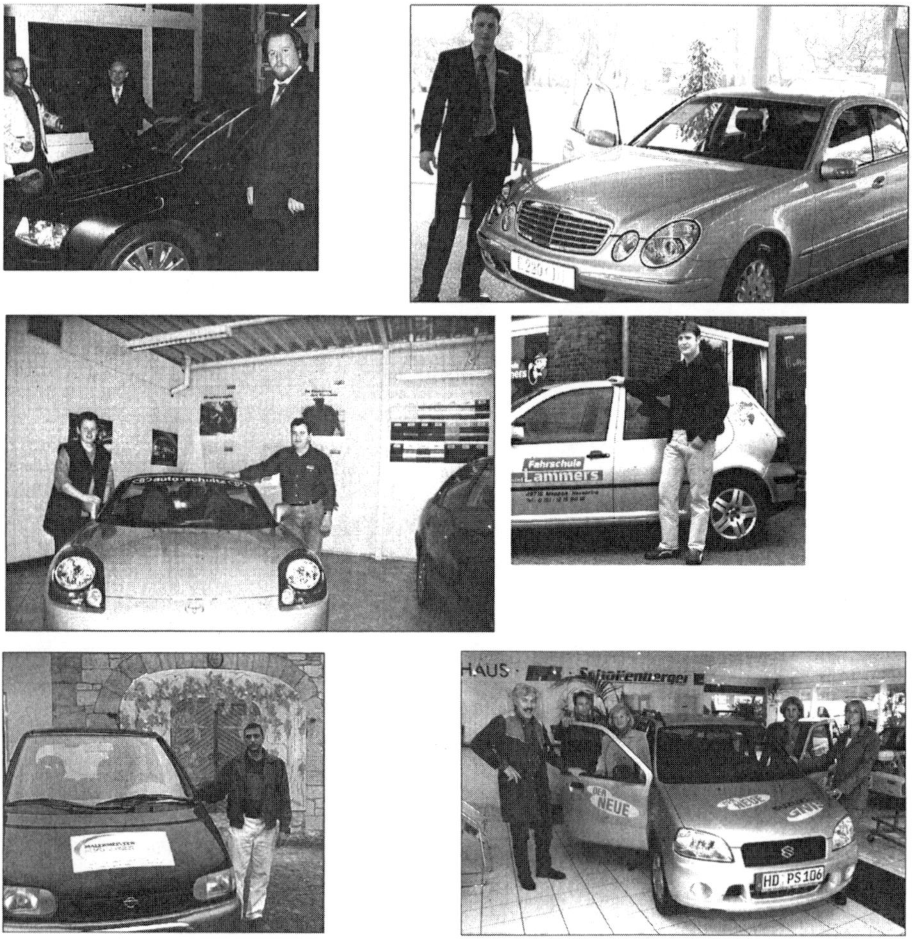

Fig. 5. Peter Piller, *Auto berühren*. Reprod. from: Christoph Keller, ed., *Archiv Peter Piller. Zeitung*, exh. cat. Salzburger Kunstverein, Hamburger Kunsthalle and Kunsthaus Glarus, Zürich 2007, n. pag. © VG Bild-Kunst, Bonn 2014.

ment of editorial content and advertising because many pictures seem to show local tradesmen. Whereas one picture of a person standing next to a car would not tell us anything, ten pictures of people and cars show certain patterns and create a context of meaning.

Next to *Auto berühren* hang seven pictures in different sizes, some in black-and-white and some in color, but it is still obvious that they belong together.

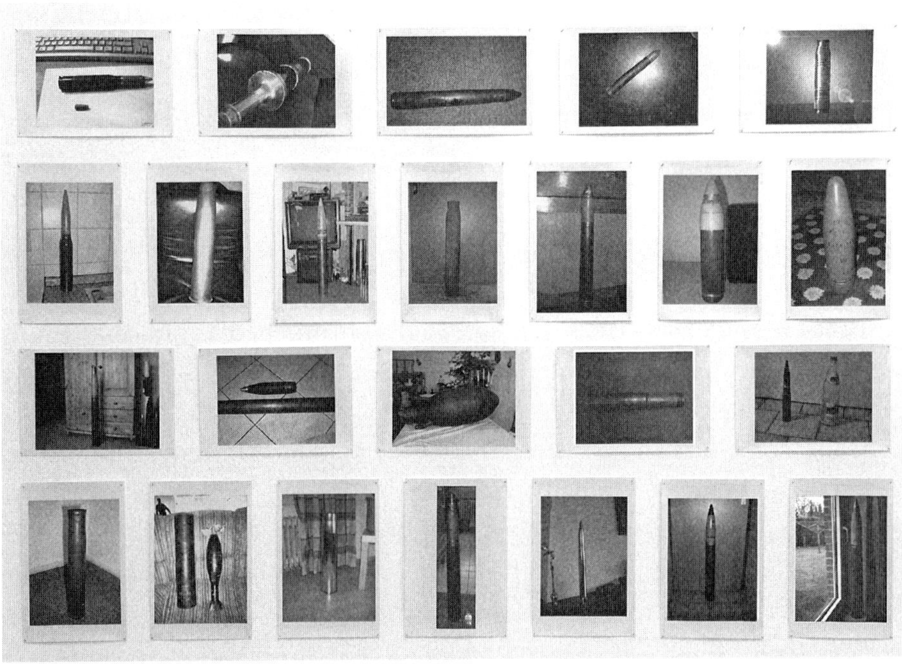

Fig. 6. Peter Piller, *Deko + Munition*, 2007, inkjet prints (installation view Salzburger Kunstverein). © Salzburger Kunstverein / VG Bild-Kunst, Bonn 2014. Photo: Andrew Phelps.

Their subject is the same: they all show young girls shooting. Because the common feature is evident at first sight, they are perceived as a group, in spite of their formal differences. Generally, one might expect the depiction of weapons with men, or at least with female soldiers or policewomen. Piller's pictures surprise by presenting young girls in casual clothes apparently shooting not for professional reasons, but for fun. Because of their original publication in regional newspapers, they remind of sport-shooting clubs[28] popular in many rural parts of Germany. On the right side of this group, there are twelve smaller pictures showing old ammunition, which were photographed in private homes (fig. 6). Piller found these pictures on

28 The German word "Schützenverein" can literally be translated as "marksmen club".

eBay, where the old projectiles are offered as collectibles. This group entitled *Deko + Munition* [decor + ammunition] also exists in the form of an artist's postcard book. To a smaller extent than *Girls Shooting*, these pictures affect the viewer because of the astonishment caused by the combination of contrarily perceived items such as weapons, young girls and home decoration.
Piller's installations encourage an active viewer. Apart from recognizing different groups of pictures by looking for a common attribute as in a picture puzzle, the viewer also builds links between the groups to find possible meanings of the overall arrangement. In this example, one can draw a line from one fetish of the German province to another; that is, from cars to shooting clubs and ammunition. Is the contemplation of Piller's installations guided in some way or is it up to the viewer to choose a direction? In the case of the emblem, it is mostly a question of moving from picture to text, or vice versa. The contemplation of an emblem can be described as circular – in the process of looking for the overall meaning, one will go back and forth between the parts. The same is true for the installations of Piller; they also work with a circular movement rather than a linear one. Because the viewer has to find the common attribute, it is not enough to regard one picture after another. After having formed an idea, it is necessary to go back and check if the attribute is present in all pictures of the group. In analogy to the shape of a circle, there is no mandatory direction of viewing – it is possible to proceed from left to right and top to bottom, or form right to left and bottom to top.
In Piller's installations, the attempt of the viewer to find a general meaning is often questioned by their ironic note and ostentatiously subjective and non-scientific criteria. By using these personal, random categories in order to arrange his material, Piller illustrates his doubts about every classification system. Piller not only encodes meaning by arranging his pictures in the style of a crossword, but with his use of irony he simultaneously challenges the possibility to create correlations that could claim objective validity.
Piller's strategy of codification is closely linked to decoding. To encode something, implies having in mind someone else to do the deciphering. Since emblems as well as installation encourage the viewer to search for the meaning, the question is whether the principle of 'to profit and to delight' can also be employed with regard to contemporary installations. Piller's pic-

tures suggest that it is fairly common to pose for a photo while touching a car, or that regional newspapers show more pictures of girls shooting than possibly expected. These are minor lessons compared to those conveyed by the emblem. These pictures provide aesthetic rather than moral insights. Through Pillers work the viewer can gain an understanding of the nature of pictures – of the standardized photographs and visual patterns in the media, but also of the value and unexpected aesthetics of trivial newspaper pictures, at least after having been edited by an artist. If the profit in its moral sense is of no importance for Piller's installations, the delight in discovering new and surprising things is, on the other hand, very present. This holds especially true because one would not have expected to discover something interesting in the triteness of newspaper photography.

*

To draw a conclusion, in the majority of contemporary installations there is no conscious reference of the artist to the emblem. But the fact remains that many installations operate with strategies of combination and codification – with emblematic strategies. Thus, the emblem can help to understand how installations work. From a different point of view, it can help to perceive aspects such as the participation of the viewer or the combination of different pieces often thought to be intrinsically tied to modern art.

Ouroboros in the Digital Age. Joan Krieger's Emblems of *Ekphrasis*

JOHANNES FRÖHLICH

In the world of Renaissance emblem studies, *digital emblematica* generally refers to digital facsimiles of these printed works. One rarely thinks of emblems as "digital natives" or "born digital." Yet nine particular emblems mark the beginnings of the emblem as computer-generated art. In 1990 Joan Krieger digitally created nine emblems to be published in Murray Krieger's *Ekphrasis: The Illusion of the Natural Sign.*[1] Eight images introduce eight chapters of Murray Krieger's scholarly work while the ninth functions as an emblem to the entire book. The images are accompanied by the chapter title and an epigraph, thereby producing tripartite emblems.[2] Thus, the title of each chapter of *Ekphrasis* can be read as the *motto* of each emblem, with the epigraph and the illustration functioning as *pictura* and *subscriptio*. The following investigation analyzes the emblematic strategies constitutive in two of Joan and Murray Krieger's emblems. The Krieger emblems represent the concept of ekphrasis within literary criticism as well as the dynamic qualities of digitally created art. The former function exploits classical European emblem motifs and formalistic structures to contextualize Murray Krieger's work. The latter comments on the temporality of art media. Thus, in anticipation of the coming digital century Joan Krieger revitalizes the concept of

1 Murray Krieger, *Ekphrasis. The Illusion of the Natural Sign*, Baltimore 1992.

2 Manning defines the three-part emblem as a "motto, a picture, and a following explanatory text." See John Manning, *The Emblem*, London 2002, 18.

emblems in a strategic way as a dynamic concept of representation in the last decade of the twentieth century.

*

Murray Krieger's *Ekphrasis* presents an overview of the different theoretical debates about ekphrases. This 1992 publication belongs to his later works, summarizing nearly thirty years of his scholarly research on ekphrases begun in 1967 with his essay "*Ekphrasis* and the Still Movement of Poetry; or *Laokoön* Revisited", and which is republished in the appendix. The *Encyclopaedia Britannica* describes Murray Krieger as an "American literary critic known for his studies of the special nature of the language of [...] imaginative literature" who also "believ[es] that poetic language has a unique capacity to reveal vision and meaning, a capacity beyond the scope of everyday language."[3] The term 'ekphrasis' often appears in an art historical, rhetorical, or literary context. The literary critic John Hollander defines the term in his entry in the *Encyclopedia of Aesthetics* as a term which "is used today in its narrower sense to mean the literary description of a work of art, usually employing considerable rhetorical art and, in a broader sense, to designate entire poems or passages from longer works of fiction, poetry, or expository essays that address in various ways particular works of painting, sculpture, graphic art, or perhaps even architecture."[4]

Quoting Leo Spitzer, Murray Krieger describes ekphrasis as "the poetic description of a pictorial or sculptural work of art [...] through the medium of words."[5] This "description", though, does not necessarily refer to an author describing an extant piece of art which exists outside the narrative. Indeed, and especially in literary contexts, most ekphrases refer to a fictional painting or sculpture within the narrative. The representation of both the object of art itself and how it is received through verbal media is characteristic of the permanent desire to see art which cannot be seen. The impossibility of seeing the narrated art works results in a feeling of unfulfilled desire which is the special quality of ekphrases – a description of an image which does not exist. In this sense an ekphrasis can be similar to what John Manning calls in his introduction to *The Emblem* a "naked emblem" – an emblem which is lacking a picture.[6]

Each chapter of *Ekphrasis* is introduced by an emblematic illustration by Joan Krieger, which collectively, as Murray Krieger's introduction explains, are designed to spell the Greek word for ekphrasis (ΕΚΦΡΑΣΙΣ). Thus, Krieger notes that his work is an imitation of the word whose concept he is describing – "an ekphrasis of an ekphrasis."[7] In this manner ekphrases and emblems are juxtaposed to elaborate on each other.

> I call them 'emblems' but they are intended as free adaptations, in modern computer graphics (composed on Macintosh SE and PC 386), of the practice of designing illuminated letters to ornament medieval manuscripts. At the beginning of each chapter below, they are balanced by my epigraphs as twin attempts (one visual, one verbal) to emblematize the discussion that follows.[8]

This key passage, or rather key footnote, provides the basis for the following analysis. Murray Krieger explains the intention behind Joan Krieger's images. The images are stylistic devices that ornament his chapters in the tradition of medieval manuscript, as well as emblematize his scholarly work. Furthermore, this footnote reveals that the emblems function collectively. The combination of Murray Krieger's epigraphs and Joan Krieger's images evokes the emblematic function. In a narrow sense, without his epigraphs and chapter titles, Joan Krieger's images remain mere illustrations. However, her designs are promoted as an essential part of the book. In his foreword Krieger writes, "each of the eight chapters of my book is introduced by the representation of an emblem shaped as a circular shield, created by Joan Krieger [...]."[9] In this manner, Murray Krieger explicitly draws attention to his own emblematic strategy.

3 "Murray Krieger", in: *Encyclopaedia Britannica. Encyclopaedia Britannica Online*, http://www.britannica.com/EBchecked/topic/323489/Murray-Krieger (accessed 10 Sept 2014).
4 John Hollander, "Ecphrasis", in: *Encyclopedia of Aesthetics*, ed. Michael Kelly, http://www.oxfordartonline.com/subscriber/article/opr/t234/e0185 (accessed 10 Sept 2014).
5 Krieger 1992 (as note 1), xiii.
6 Manning 2002 (as note 2), 18.
7 Krieger 1992 (as note 1), xiv.
8 Krieger 1992 (as note 1), xiv.
9 Krieger 1992 (as note 1), xiii-xiv.

Joan Krieger composed her emblems virtually on Macintosh SE and PC 386.[10] While her approach shows how the emblems' structure is flexible enough to adapt to new media and technologies, in this case, the modern computer example of emblem design illustrates how the medium itself influences our reception. The emblem design confirms its modern and digital approach, while it adapts classical motifs like the snake Ouroboros, the double theater masks of antiquity, or historic musical instruments.[11] They do not imitate copper plates or wood cuts but adapt certain characteristics of their structural design. All nine emblems are in black and white and circular. This stark black and white contrast has no grey gradations. Joan Krieger engenders the impression of a wood cut, whereby shadows are created through a combination of black and white pixels. The reduced coloration compensates for the lack of a spatial perspective by the creation of patterns and the juxtaposition of objects.

*

The most striking emblem in this book is the Ouroboros emblem; the snake representing eternity (fig. 1). Readers must observe this emblem before they start reading Murray Krieger's *Ekphrasis*. As with the other emblems designed by Joan Krieger, Ouroboros is portrayed in a circular shield. Three circles surround the entwined serpent. Like other snakes, Ouroboros is naturally limbless, though it is portrayed with two wings like a dragon. The outer circle, like the inner circle, is entirely black. The circle framed by these two black circles is white and has a pattern which reminds the readers/viewers of the crests of waves or a snakeskin. The serpent's body is scaled, with the scales arranged in two different patters. The dominant pattern of the scale structure does not follow the natural form of the curved body. Like most of Joan Krieger's patterns, the scale structure envelops the serpent's body like foil with variations to create the illusion of depth. A secondary less dominant scale structure imitates honeycombs that define Ouroboros' body in the background. This contrast, in turn, results in the creation of perspec-

10 See Krieger 1992 (as note 1), xiv.

11 See Krieger 1992 (as note 1), e.g. ii, 30, 233.

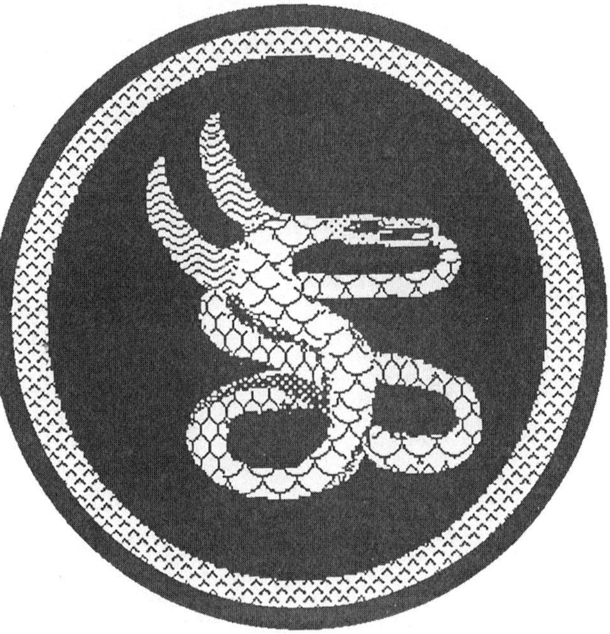

The *ouroboros*, emblem of the alchemical *prima materia*, holder of the secret of the universe

> "The visual emblem and the verbal emblem are complementary languages for seeking the representation of the unrepresentable. Ekphrasis is the poet's marriage of the two within the verbal art." P. 22

Fig. 1. Joan Krieger, no title. Reprod. from: Murray Krieger. Ekphrasis: The Illusion of the Natural Sign. p. ii. © 1992 The Johns Hopkins University Press. Reprinted with permission of Johns Hopkins University Press.

tive. This simplified version of space seems neither related to Renaissance linear perspective, nor to modern photographic perspective. It is instead an example of modernist illustrations or bas-reliefs. Further, Joan Krieger creates the illusion of depth in her emblem by adding shadow-structures in the form of black and white dot combinations, though the former dominate the shadow. The wings of Ouroboros have a rhythmic wave pattern like sine curves, while the creature's beak-like mouth devours its own tail. Thus, Krieger's adaptation of this traditional emblem motif preserves many of its traditional characteristics, such as the devouring of the tail and the serpentine body.

In many earlier renditions of this popular motif, the figure of Ouroboros is either part of a complex composition or itself a circular frame. Ouroboros traditionally seems to frame an essential concept, and adds the component of eternity to a scene, an idea, or an object. A variation in this formal approach becomes evident in Joan Krieger's adaptation, for her snake does not form a circle. One aesthetic explanation could be that the snake could have formed a fourth circle and that the resultant dominant, black center would have created a compositional imbalance. Beyond this purely formalistic explanation, a different layer of meaning becomes evident. The snake's body hides the center of the emblem; moreover, it disguises an empty space. This hidden, empty space is lacking an object. An emblem visualizing a book called *Ekphrasis* should present an image of an ekphrasis in its center, yet this is precisely the crux of the matter, since an ekphrasis cannot be visualized without losing its meaning. In other words, it is possible to draw a version of an image which an ekphrastic poem describes, but it is impossible to create an image of the ekphrastic poem itself because, by definition, ekphrases are texts and not paintings. Consequently, an infinite number of possible images can be imagined. Instead of presenting this blank Krieger decided to let the serpent's body cover the empty space as a symbol of the eternal impossibility of representation. To make this even more evident, the serpent's coiled (and not circular) shape hints at the possibly infinite number of images with its body. If one follows the line along the curvature of the tail, the infinity symbol becomes visible.

*

The emblem picture is accompanied by two epigraphs. The first, written in a smaller font, states: “The *ouroboros,* emblem of the alchemical *prima materia,* holder of the secret of the universe.” Here, then, the serpent embodies the idea of a hidden, secret knowledge, thereby expanding readers’ reception of the emblem’s background. The blackness of the inner circle and main background becomes the blackness and endlessness of the universe. The second epigraph is a quotation from Murray Krieger’s first chapter: “The visual emblem and the verbal emblem are complementary languages for seeking the representation of the unrepresentable. Ekphrasis is the poet’s marriage of the two within the verbal art.”[12] Murray Krieger expresses here that an ekphrasis is a combination of a visual and a verbal emblem. The Ouroboros image serves in this context as the visual component, while the verbal components are the epigraphs. By definition, an ekphrasis is a verbal representation of a visual object of art. Thus, by digitally creating a piece of art which represents hidden knowledge and, moreover, represents the oxymoron of visualizing the concept of ekphrasis, Joan Krieger overcomes the boundaries of the motif of the ‘Ouroboros’ and accomplishes Murray Krieger’s definition. This emblem not only symbolizes the concept ‘ekphrasis’ but it also represents the theoretical debates about, as Murray Krieger puts it, “the unrepresentable.” Nevertheless, the Ouroboros emblem gives rise to this meaning only in this specific context. The elevated position as title page and the defining epigraphs present the serpent in the tradition of title engravings in Renaissance books. Thus, the readers’ knowledge about printing traditions and the specific content of the book shape the meaning of the serpent’s body, which in turn slowly reveals the hidden knowledge behind *Ekphrasis.*

*

The second emblem in this analysis is the letter emblem for chapter 5 with the *motto* “The verbal emblem I: Renaissance” (fig. 2).[13] Murray Krieger quotes a different source for each epigraph. His epigraphs cite Shakespeare

12 Krieger 1992 (as note 1), ii.
13 Krieger 1992 (as note 1), 114.

plays, poems, or, as in this case, a humanistic work – three paragraphs from *Icones Symbolicae* by the art historian E. H. Gombrich.[14] Krieger's fifth chapter describes how during the Middle Ages and the Renaissance the written word became more important in comparison to the spoken language. The transformation of the spoken word into a visible manifestation (the written letter) created the foundation for an aesthetic of the printed, painted, or written word. Throughout the Middle Ages and the Renaissance, books were vessels for knowledge and, given their often rich and elaborate decoration with gold, diamonds, and color as well as their physical value – they were also works of art.[15] Furthermore, Krieger mentions the importance of the "especially enriched" and "highly colored" initial letters which turn into an enigmatic emblem.[16] Similarly, he writes about his letter emblems that they are designed in the tradition of illuminated letters which ornament medieval manuscripts.[17]

Joan Krieger's emblem for chapter 5 portrays a man sitting in front of a stretched canvas. His left hand supports his right hand that holds a pen. The room is dim causing the white canvas to glow. The artist wears Renaissance-style clothes and has an optical device in front of his right eye, presumably to aid him in seeing his drawing in detail. The letter "A" from the Greek word for ekphrasis is painted in a large form on the canvas. The moment portrayed shows how the artist draws fine lines for the background of his illustration. A shadow made of white and black pixels falls on the canvas. The light in the room illuminates his face. His eyes focus on his art. Between the canvas and the artist stands a small inkbottle. The painter does not hold a palette – thus, even the image within Krieger's emblem emphasizes the lack of color and employs stark black and white contrast. The letter "A" becomes the most important object in the painting. The transformation of an abstract vowel from a sound to the written letter is the content of the painting. Additionally, the canvas does not present a manuscript with an illuminated initial letter.

14 Ernst H. Gombrich, "Icones symbolicae. The visual image in neo-platonic thought", in: *Journal of the Warburg and Courtauld Institutes* 11 (1948), 163-192.

15 Krieger 1992 (as note 1), 115-116.

16 Krieger 1992 (as note 1), 116.

17 See Krieger 1992 (as note 1), xiv.

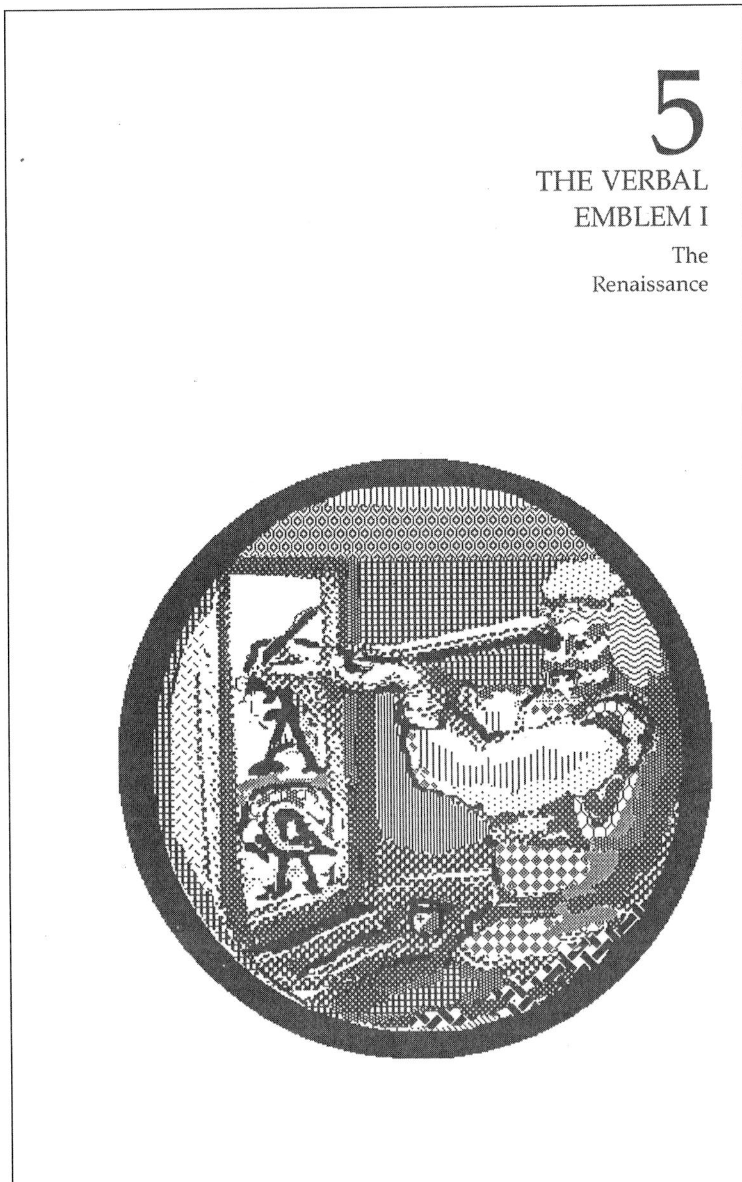

Fig. 2. Joan Krieger, no title. Reprod. from: Murray Krieger. Ekphrasis: The Illusion of the Natural Sign. p. 114. © 1992 The Johns Hopkins University Press. Reprinted with permission of Johns Hopkins University Press.

In this point Joan Krieger goes beyond the idea of the importance of the initial letter because her "A" is worthy of being presented as the only letter on the canvas. Thus, she embeds a meta-commentary on her own work as emblem artist within her emblem.

Though the references between chapter, title, and illustration seem clear, the accompanying epigraph by E.H. Gombrich challenges the coherent structure:

> Thus the mysterious hieroglyph of the monster devouring itself sets the mind a puzzle which forces it to rise above image. Not only can we not think of the sign as representing a real creature, even the event it represents transcends the possibility of our experience – what will happen when the devouring jaws reach the neck and the jaws themselves? It is this paradoxical nature of the image that has made it the archetypal symbol of mystery. We are certainly not tempted to confuse the painted enigma with its manifold meanings [...].[18]

E. H. Gombrich refers in this paragraph to Ouroboros as "the monster devouring itself." The chosen epigraph does not speak of initial letters, the Renaissance, or the process of painting. In contrast, the description refers to the first emblem, the Ouroboros emblem, thus contradicting the expectations of the readers. Gombrich points out that the enigmatic Ouroboros, without mentioning the serpent's actual name, challenges the human mind. It is neither a real creature nor is its action possibly imaginable. In other words, the idea of Ouroboros goes beyond words and beyond imagination. It is impossible to represent this idea fully. By evoking the image of the snake reaching its jaw, Gombrich pushes the concept to its limits. Thus, he concludes that "the painted enigma" and "its manifold meanings" are two different aspects. Gombrich's words emphasize that context determines how viewers behold and understand an image. While Ouroboros and a heart can signify eternal love, Ouroboros next to a book entitled *Ekphrasis* represents the impossibility of visualizing ekphrases; and, finally, an epigraph about the Ouroboros juxtaposed to an emblem about enigmatic initial letters binds Chapter 5 to the emblem representing the entire book. Joan Krieger's adaptations refer

[18] See Krieger 1992 (as note 1), 115.

to each other and the texts they represent. More importantly, though, is that her motifs – Ouroboros, the artist, or the Greek masks – mirror the long tradition of emblems and emblem motifs. The 'artist' in her emblem is not a modern artist, in spite of having been designed in a modern medium. By transforming this motif into a modern emblem, Krieger demonstrates the role of the written letter in the Renaissance and, ultimately, presents the importance of the Renaissance emblem and emblematic strategies for current discourses of text and image.

*

Yet, both Ouroboros and the artist emblem could easily be replaced with a traditional Renaissance emblem. Murray Krieger's text gives an account of the function of the images as emblem adaptations and as illuminated manuscript letters but offers no explanation for the graphic design, other than naming two electronic devices in his above-mentioned footnote. Krieger mentions in parenthesis that the "free adaptations" are "composed on Macintosh SE and PC 386." Placing this information in a footnote, and parenthetically no less, creates the impression that it has little information value. Nonetheless, it is surprising that Krieger names two electronic devices but no software program, because the image is composed only by means of the program, not the computer. The readers receive the information about the computers, the place of creation, and the approximate date of composing the image. The latter two points are mentioned in his acknowledgments when he thanks the Bellagio Study and Conference Center in Italy where "during five marvelous weeks in the spring of 1990, the bulk of this work was brought close to its final form and most of the emblems were conceived and executed."[19] The emblem as "conceived and executed" digital art bears an implicit tension and evokes the impression of distancing the art from the artist. Thus, it is fruitful to consider the capabilities and limitations of computer generated art at the beginning of the last decade of the twentieth century in order to "illuminate" Joan Krieger's letter emblems.

19 Krieger 1992 (as note 1), x.

Emblems created in 1990 are considered exceptionally recent in the field of emblem studies.[20] However, considering that such emblems were digitally designed, in turn, makes them "archaic" in the field of computer science. In this sense, Joan Krieger's emblems represent the start of computer-generated art and must therefore be understood in their historical context. Timothy Blinkley explains in his 1990 article "Digital Dilemma" the problems inherent to computerized image-making.[21] He elaborates: "we draw a picture without making a mark, wield brushes that have no bristles, mix paints that do not pour, model objects without any matter, illuminate them with dimensionless lights that never burn out [...]."[22] This description of the making of digital art shows the alienation of the creative process. The new medium and its software provide digital tools that imitate traditional artistic tools without offering the same precision. Binkley further says that a digital image does not exist as such and that the only way to capture it and make it physical is to print it.[23] Following this line of argumentation means that the emblems in Murray Krieger's book are digitally created images but not digital images. They are printed versions of software-generated images. Thus, Joan Krieger's actual emblems are absent in the printed text, and readers can only observe a transformed version of her art.

Even without Murray Krieger's footnote it seems obvious for modern readers that the emblems are digitally created. The pixelated structure and the lack of depth betray an early stage of graphic design. The 1990 article disproves the contemporary readers' assumption when Binkley states: "The fact that the screen shows an array of individual dots called "pixels" might be taken as evidence confirming the digital nature of the picture. The coarse mosaic of most early computer images was once considered a telltale sign of computer involvement, for better or worse." As early as in his 1990 article Binkley

20 See for example Peter M. Daly, "The *Nachleben* of the Emblem in Some Modern Logos, Advertisements, and Propaganda", in: *Companion to Emblem Studies*, ed. Peter M. Daly, New York 2008, 489-517.

21 See Timothy Binkley, "Digital Dilemma", in: Pamela Grant-Ryan et al., eds., *Leonardo. Journal of the International Society for the Arts, Sciences and Technology*, Supplemental Issue (1990), 13-19.

22 Binkley 1990 (as note 21), 13.

23 Binkley 1990 (as note 21), 13.

defines visible pixels as a "telltale sign of computer involvement." Rethinking Krieger's images, it becomes clear that she used pixels as a specific technique of alienation. The enlarged pixels make the recognition of the depicted object more difficult, challenging readers' perception. This consciously applied indicator of "computer involvement" creates its own independent aesthetics, especially because Krieger's emblems are specifically designed for a book. This fact makes it impossible to assume that, for example, with enough distance the pixels might blur into one coherent image – but Krieger's pixels remain pixels. Furthermore, the digital approach enables the images to be more closely related to the text than traditional methods of illustration. Medieval manuscripts are illustrated by hand, not printed, and therefore unique and inseparably related to the individual manuscript. Modern publication practices, in contrast, digitally incorporate scanned images into books. Keeping the digital origin visible, then, shows that Krieger's images were copied as a data file into the text file of *Ekphrasis*. In this way, the graphic design allows a "medieval" understanding of text-image relations in the era of mass-reproduction. The images only belong to this text.

A further problem with computer-generated art in 1990 – even in 2014 – is that, as Roger F. Malina describes: "In computer arts the artwork itself, embedded in digital data and software, is not directly accessible to the human senses."[24] Computer art is always mediated and cannot be touched. Thus, it remains inaccessible; it remains unavailable to human senses. Malina further elaborates that computers are not designed for artists. He states: "The computer keyboard, mouse, digitizing tablet are all inferior tools for drawing compared to a piece of charcoal."[25] The problem as described by Malina in 1990 has not changed in recent years. In 2006 Malina refers to the same problem when he states that "Even today's handheld and wearable devices are essentially foreign objects to the body and mind of the user. [...] The deep desire to achieve this kind of seamless and multimodal integration can be seen in various initiatives in ubiquitous, pervasive, and wearable comput-

24 Roger F. Malina, "Digital Image–Digital Cinema: The Work of Art in the Age of Post-Mechanical Reproduction", in: Grant-Ryan et al. 1990 (as note 21), 33-38, here 33.

25 Malina 1990 (as note 24), 34.

ing; clearly the computer is only just beginning to enter the biological age."[26] The ongoing desire to overcome imperfection leads to a dynamic understanding of computer art. However, bearing in mind that Krieger's emblems are free adaptations of emblems, the graphic design reminds the reader in this modern context of the relation between the woodcut and the engraving. A standard of perfect imitation is nearly impossible to attain within the art of woodcuts. Thus, the letter emblems also comment on the discourse of *ut pictura poesis* and abandon the need for perfect imitation. Hence, referencing the illustrated object is adequate for a modern aesthetics.

In addition to the insufficient tools for creating computer-designed art, the vulnerability of software is a further disadvantage.[27] Software can always be changed and is an example of a dynamic and never ending process of creating. In contrast, traditional forms of art are static. It would be possible to paint another layer of color on a painting but that would be just another layer and not a substantial change. Therefore, creating the emblems digitally promotes a dynamic understanding of art and the multiplicity of representation. This dynamic is, of course, only implied in the printed version. The dynamic process is implicit and represented in the data file, which contains the "original." Ultimately, the mutability of the image propels visual art beyond its static boundaries and lends it a dynamic quality inherent to literature.

Krieger's decision to present her ideas in a pixel-design, which was already outdated in 1990, can be read as an awareness of development and progress. The concept of emblems is adaptable to new media as shown in the printed image and will further change and adapt in the future. Thus, her emblems represent the transfer of knowledge into new media and, consequently, represent the digital emblem as container of memory as the most important quality of her aesthetics.[28] The patterns and dots are a conscious artistic strategy enveloping the past and the present. The patterns create an image, but, moreover, they show an adapted emblem, as well as adapted pixels. The

26 Roger F. Malina, "A Forty-Year Perspective on Aesthetic Computing in the *Leonardo Journal*", in: *Aesthetic Computing*, ed. Paul Fishwick, Cambridge 2006, 43-52, here 44-45.

27 See Malina 1990 (as note 24).

28 See Michael Leyton, "The Foundations of Aesthetics", in: Fishwick 2006 (as note 26), 289-313. The theory that the rules of aesthetics are the rules of memory storage is developed by Michael Leyton in the broad field of Aesthetic Computing.

illuminated canvas in the emblem of the artist becomes the computer screen that shows an abstract object without embodiment – the "A."

*

In conclusion, the analysis shows that Joan Krieger's images function as modern emblems introducing each chapter of Murray Krieger's book. The collaborative work of Murray and Joan Krieger creates three-part-emblems consisting of the chapter title as *motto*, the image as *pictura*, and the epigraph as *subscriptio*. The Ouroboros emblem, a meta-emblem for the entire book, illustrates the concept of the "unrepresentable" ekphrases within the visual arts. Furthermore, the specific design of computer-generated images visualizes the adaptability of emblems on the one hand, and the aesthetics of transferring knowledge on the other. Hence, the illustrations exemplify the transformation of art forms and confirm that new media reinterpret preexisting art forms. Joan Krieger's emblems are designed to inform readers about the past and suggest the evolving dynamics of contemporary art. Finally, Joan Krieger composed emblems that mirror the concept of *Ekphrasis*, as well as the *Illusion of the Natural Sign*, thereby embodying the intellectual conceptualization of Murray Krieger's study.

Words and Images.
Emblematic Aspects in Object Art of the 1960s

CHRISTINE KORTE-BEUCKERS

Within the 1960s, there was a revolutionary change in contemporary art. Whereas the art of the 1950s has to be regarded in relation to the situation of the cultural disaster after the Second World War, as a phase of introspection which the Art Informel reflects in its retreat to an inner space of feelings and individual expressions, it is the art of the upcoming 1960s that came to terms with the past.
This renewal shows a consideration of different traditions in imageries and the aim for reaching new ways. It leads to the questions whether emblematic strategies are pursued in contemporary art of that time, to what extent and in which ways.
The following ideas on emblematic structures are based on selected criteria concerning the question what lets pictures appear as emblems. Therefore, three different categories were selected: first, a structural formal category, second, a functional category, and third, a characterizing category concerned with the impact or effect. These three criteria could also be summarized in the questions: How are they made? What are they for? And what are they like? As to the structural category, it seems important whether a tripartite composition has been chosen, dividing the pieces of art into the three characteristic parts of *lemma* or *motto*, of *icon* or *pictura*, and of *epigram* or *subscriptio*. The first part introduces the topic, the second part serves to illustrate the content, and the third part adds further explanations to the topic or broadens it. Next to the basic formal construction of the emblem, its functional quality is concerned with the comparability of emblematic functions

such as their moralizing aim and their entertaining, amusing or edifying purpose. The third category questions noticeable features or attitudes – for example, in a narrative, illustrative and exemplifying kind of art.

*

A prevalent idea of the 1960s was to break with the past, an idea that deeply influenced all contemporary art movements. In order to set art free in a new way, former ties to the past had to be loosened, and borders overcome. This process could be observed, for example, in the handling of materials showing a growing interest in new technical products, in the use of commodities of everyday life, and in art's extension into new dimensions of space, time and immateriality.

Within those innovative art concepts of the 1960s, classical genres are explicitly given up clearing the way for more innovative art concepts. Crossovers of art, music and theatre create new forms, for example, in the Happening and Fluxus movements. Minimal Art even entails a shift from an optical to an intellectual notion of pictures. The idea of attitudes becoming form was summarized in the title of a legendary exhibition at the *Kunsthalle Bern* in 1968 organized by Harald Szeeman which represents the understanding of art at that time.[1] The attitude was to reach into the center of consciousness.[2]

The literary movement of Lettrism, originally a French avant-garde movement and established in Paris in the 1940s by Isidore Isou, gave significant impetus for the art scene. This movement attributed an important relevance to words and slogans. They were freed from their ties to coherence and set, and, with view to surrealistic ideas, were transferred into new haphazard contexts. In his thesis of *hypergraphology*, Isou expedited the liberation of letters and the replacement of pictures and figures by words, letters and signs. Thus, words became part of pictures.[3]

1 *Live in your head. When Attitudes Become Form. Works-Concepts-Processes-Situations-Information*, exh. cat. Kunsthalle Bern, ed. Harald Szeemann, Bern 1969.

2 See Karin Stempel, "Mythos 68 oder die Logik der Primzahlen", in: *'68 – Kunst und Kultur*, ed. Burkhard Leismann, Cologne 1993, 12-27, here 25.

Emerging from Lettrism, it has primarily been the Situationist International to take great influence on the avant-garde art movement since the late 1950s. This international organization of social revolutionaries, which merged avant-garde artists like Ansgar Jorn, intellectuals, and political theorists such as the filmmaker Guy Debord, was active until its dissolution in 1972. It reached the climax of its creative output and influence in 1967 and 1968 with two most significant texts *The Society of the Spectacle* by Guy Debord and *The Revolution of Everyday Life* by Raoul Vaneigem.[4] The mixture of politically aimed ideas and expressed writing, which can be found in other Situationist publications as well, proved great influence in shaping the ideas behind the May 1968 insurrections in France. Quotes, phrases and slogans from Situationist's texts and publications expressing rather poetic and happening-like ideas than propaganda or militant action,[5] were ubiquitous on posters and graffiti throughout France during the uprisings.[6]

Some of the appellative characters of the new art concepts in the 1960s were based on these influences and created new pictorial strategies incorporating interdisciplinary and intermedial ideas, which were formed by linguistic images and inspired by political agitation. The increasing influence of press photography even brought about the combining of images and phrases.

One of the most important and influential scandal press photos relating to the 1968 students' revolution was taken by photographers in 1967 during the transfer of the presidency of the University of Hamburg from Karl-Heinz

3 See Mirelle Bandini, *Pour une histoire du lettrisme*, Paris 2003. – Fabrice Flahutez, *Le lettrisme historique était une avant-garde*, Paris 2011. – For hypergraphology see Roland Sabatier, *Figures D'Isidore Isou*, in: http://www.rolandsabatier.com/0/isou.html (accessed 10 September 2014).

4 Guy Debord, *La société du spectacle*, Paris 1967. – Raoul Vaneigem, *Traité du savoir-vivre à l'usage des jeunes générations*, Paris 1967.

5 See Jean Jacques Lebel, "Die Dadaisierung des Politischen", in: *Um 1968. Konkrete Utopien in Kunst und Gesellschaft*, exh. cat. Städtische Kunsthalle Düsseldorf, ed. Marie Luise Syring, Cologne 1990, 49–52, here 49.

6 For Situationist International see *In girum imus nocte et consumimur igni. Die Situationistische Internationale (1957–1972)*, exh. cat. Museum Tinguely Basel, eds. Stefan Zweifel, Juri Steiner and Heinz Stahlhut, Zürich 2007. – Max Jakob Orlich, *Situationistische Internationale. Eintritt, Austritt, Ausschluss. Zur Dialektik interpersoneller Beziehungen und Theorieproduktion einer ästhetisch-politischen Avantgarde (1957–1972)*, Bielefeld 2011.

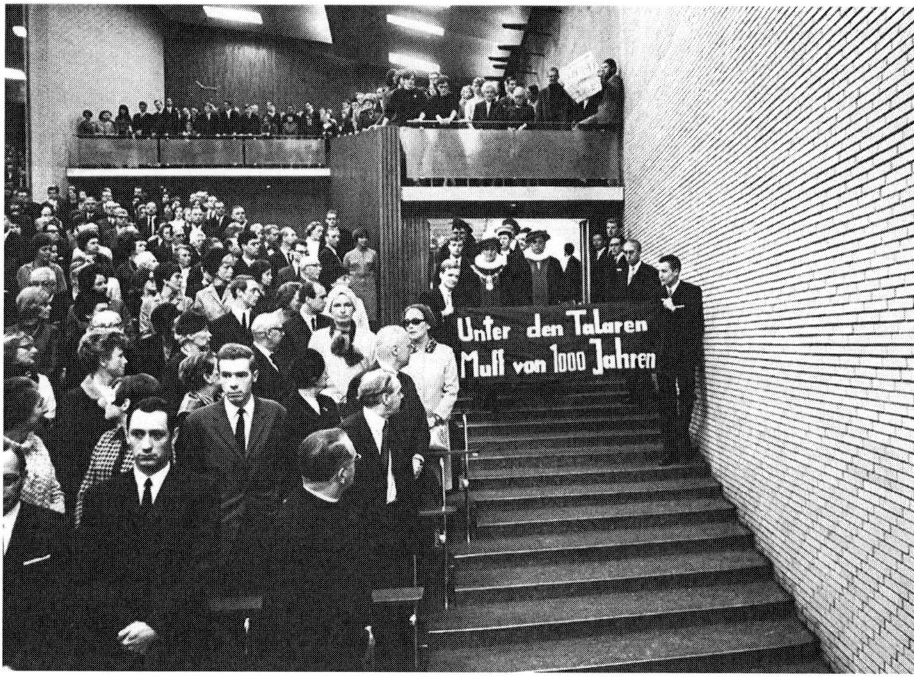

Fig. 1. Press photograph, Hamburg November 9, 1967. © Deutsche Presseagentur.

Schäfer to Werner Ehrlicher (fig. 1). Leading the procession, the students Gert Hinnerk Behlmer and Detlev Albers unrolled a banner so that the professors were not able to see it. However, the press was able to take a range of pictures. It caused a great stir among the guests as soon as the robed professors entered the official celebration hall with the transparent in front of them.[7]

The slogan on the transparent said "Unter den Talaren / Muff von 1000 Jahren". It related to the missing reappraisal of the national socialistic past and criticized obsolete totalitarian structures within the university system

[7] For the incident see Uwe Bahnsen, "Unter den Talaren Muff von 1000 Jahren. Ein Plakat geht um die Welt. Ex-Staatsrat Gert Hinnerk Behlmer provozierte damals die Universität", in: *Die Welt* 12.11.2007 [http://www.welt.de/welt_print/article1354405/Unter-den-Talaren-Muff-von-1000-Jahren-Ein-Plakat-geht-um-die-Welt.html (accessed 10 September 2014)].

still suppressing students. This slogan had become an essential catch phrase which was carried further through the entire movement and has been quoted many times. Beside a significant number of anti-imperialistic slogans and paroles which had been carried out in the youth demonstrations in Liège (Belgium) in the same year,[8] it was exactly that slogan to remain in people's consciousness as it was connected to the publicity of a press photo. Influential combinations of words and images like these certainly influenced artists to take up words and slogans in their artworks which put them in a certain tradition of the bimedial structure of emblematic pictures. Another source for the combination of words and pictures could be found in the rising importance of press reports on television and in papers. The opening up of art to everyday issues, which can be observed in the widespread movements of Nouveau Réalisme and Pop Art, allowed everyday news to become art. The combination of headlines or slogans and pictures fostered stronger mental impulses and entered into the public's mind. Increasingly, advertisements and commercials as well as the new propaganda press – as a sign of a new critical public consciousness – forced these forms of picture-slogan-combinations. It also marks the beginning of an extensively documented event culture in which incidents were kept in photos, fixed in words and commented or condensed in slogans. Strategies for an intellectually easily digestible presentation of events were consciously developed.
In the following, different exemplary and selected art positions are chosen in order to discuss new artistic procedures of the combination of words and pictures in art.

*

A highly politically motivated artist to work with slogans within his objects was Hans Peter Alvermann. He was born in Düsseldorf in 1931. As a member of the German communist party (KPD), he had straight political aims he tried to transport through his objects, and between 1966 and 1970 he extensively interrupted his work as an artist for his political commitment. He

8 See Lebel 1990 (as note 5), 50.

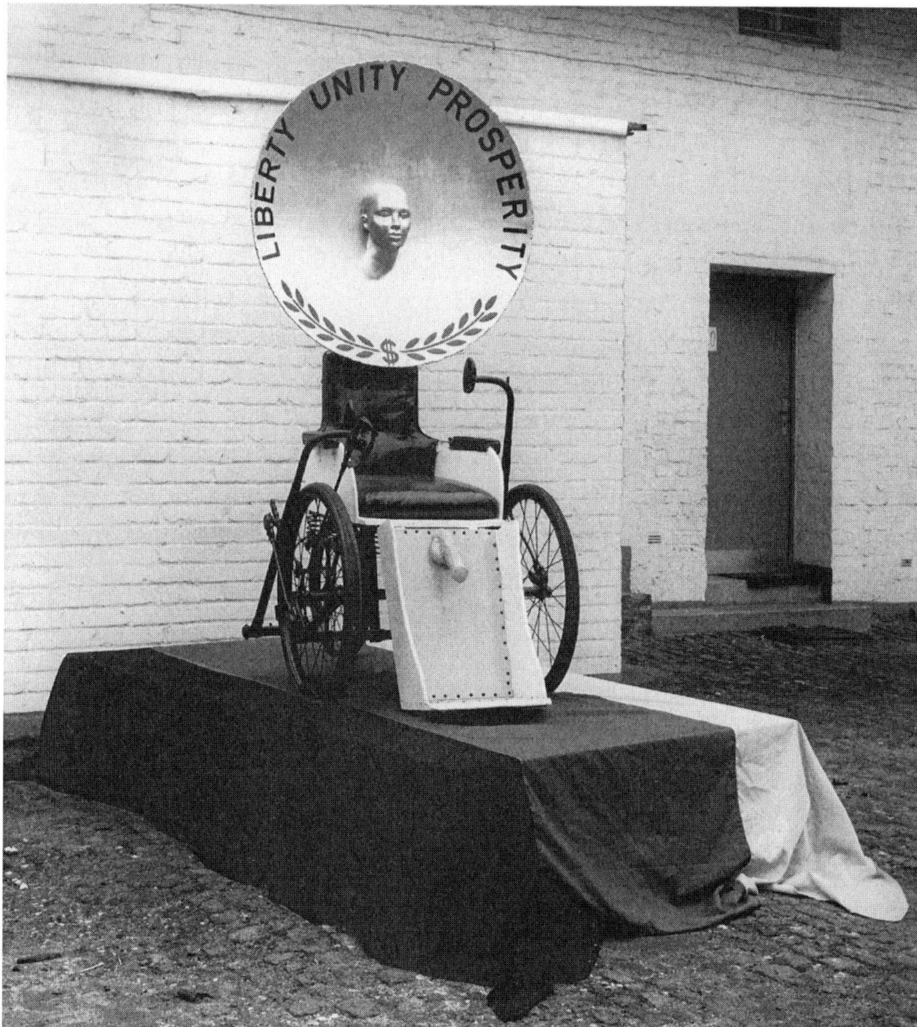

Fig. 2. Hans Peter Alvermann, *Liberty – Unity – Prosperity*, 1965 (WV 93). Kunstpalast Düsseldorf (Dauerleihgabe im Germanischen Nationalmuseum Nürnberg). © VG Bild-Kunst, Bonn 2014. Photo: Archiv Hans Peter Alvermann, Düsseldorf.

organized the republic club in Düsseldorf, forced the protest against the emergency law and the war in Vietnam.[9]

Alvermann is well known for his assemblage objects. His work is expressively realistic and points to social criticism and political themes.[10] Many of his objects show the combination of images taken from items of everyday life and inscriptions referring to this thematic relationship. In 1965 he created an object titled *Liberty – Unity – Prosperity* (fig. 2).[11] It shows a rostrum covered with the German flag. Placed upon it, is a wheelchair with male genitals attached to it, and something like a big coin forms a halo to the non-individual face of a dummy in the middle. The words are inscribed in the halo.

From an emblematic perspective, this title captioning the monument could be seen to some extent as a *lemma* or *inscriptio* to the icon, which is more than a title. While a title is usually something separate from the object itself, in this work it becomes an explicit part of the staging. It is the subject, the verbal image, which is characterized in the assemblage object in a three-dimensional picture. In this notion, the three basic ideals liberty, unity and prosperity to which the work has reference seem to have lost their aura of respectability. As expressed by the wheelchair, they are shown to be disabled. Furthermore, they are inhuman, without a trace of individual mankind which is expressed by the head of a shop dummy, and combined with the male genitals as a sign of blank potency.[12] The body of the figure as the substance of being and corporeality is missing.

The *epigram*, as the third part of the emblematic structure, seems to be missing at first sight. But if the function of the *epigram* consists in an explaining role to *icon* and *lemma*, this function is indeed transferred in a different way, because this artwork refers to another piece of artwork. The artwork is meant to be an ironic hint towards the Lincoln Memorial in Washington, which, two years earlier in 1963, even in Germany had become famous for the anti-war demonstrations and the speech of Martin Luther King at that place, beginning with the glorious words "I have a dream". These words had become the quintessence of a fight for humanity, peace and equality. It refers

9 For the biography of Alvermann see *Kunst und Politik*, exh. cat. Badischer Kunstverein Karlsruhe, ed. Georg Bussmann, Karlsruhe 1969.

10 See Stephan von Wiese, "Zu den Skulpturen von Hans Peter Alvermann", in: *Hans Peter Alvermann*, exh. cat. Kunstmuseum Düsseldorf, eds. Stephan von Wiese and Johannes auf der Lake, Düsseldorf 1988, 6. – Christine Korte-Beuckers, *Kommunikationskonzepte in der Objektkunst der 1960er Jahre am Beispiel ausgewählter Arbeiten* [...] (Theorie der Gegenwartskunst, vol. 13), Münster et. al. 1999, 41–75.

11 See exh. cat. Düsseldorf 1988 (as note 10), 21.

12 See von Wiese 1988 (as note 10), 9.

to this monument not only in the adapted composition, but also in the choice of the English title from which the words were taken. As a result, here the comment is not primarily given by words inside the vision, but evoked by an imaginary cross-reference of images, ideas and even of those famous words as an explaining link conserved in man's collective consciousness. Lincoln himself became a symbol of the fight for equality which in his case was the uprising against slavery. Ideas of the peace movement and anti-capitalism confronted and questioned new economic aims and values.

Accordingly, Alvermann's work has to be seen as an ironic statement towards the glory and the misery of society and state. In a capitalistically organized and post-World War society, money becomes the symbol for mankind's potency. In this society, people are no longer sitting well-dressed in armchairs, but they are cripples with their inner values being replaced by money. In this way, Alvermann's object can be seen as a form of an ideogram: it shows a transformation of statements into a visualization, which makes it analogue to epigrams.

The ostentatious character of Alvermann's art brings out a new quality and refers to the public. At first, there is a feeling of art being a medium to show social responsibility in a way of disagreement with common rules, law and the government itself.

In a way, this kind of politically inspired art is a taking up of ideas that have already been prepared in the Dada movement after the First World War. Even the collage strategies and the inclusion of words were common in that movement, which originally was primarily a literary movement. For example, this is visible in the artworks of the German artist Kurt Schwitters, a very important member and creator of the Hanoverian Dada movement, who often used words cut out of papers in his collages. In his work, words are not only dropped into the picture, but he is also playing with words and meanings taken out of their original context in order to create a new one.[13] Schwitters had already in 1920 created assemblage objects, for example *Heilige Bekümmernis*, in which he added slogans to a combined object out

[13] See Dietmar Elger, "Die Worte und die Bilder. Beispiele der Integration von Schrift in die bildende Kunst", in: *In other words. Wort und Schrift in Bildern der konzeptionellen Kunst*, exh. cat. Museum am Ostwall Dortmund, ed. Anna Meseure, Stuttgart 1989, 88-93, here 90.

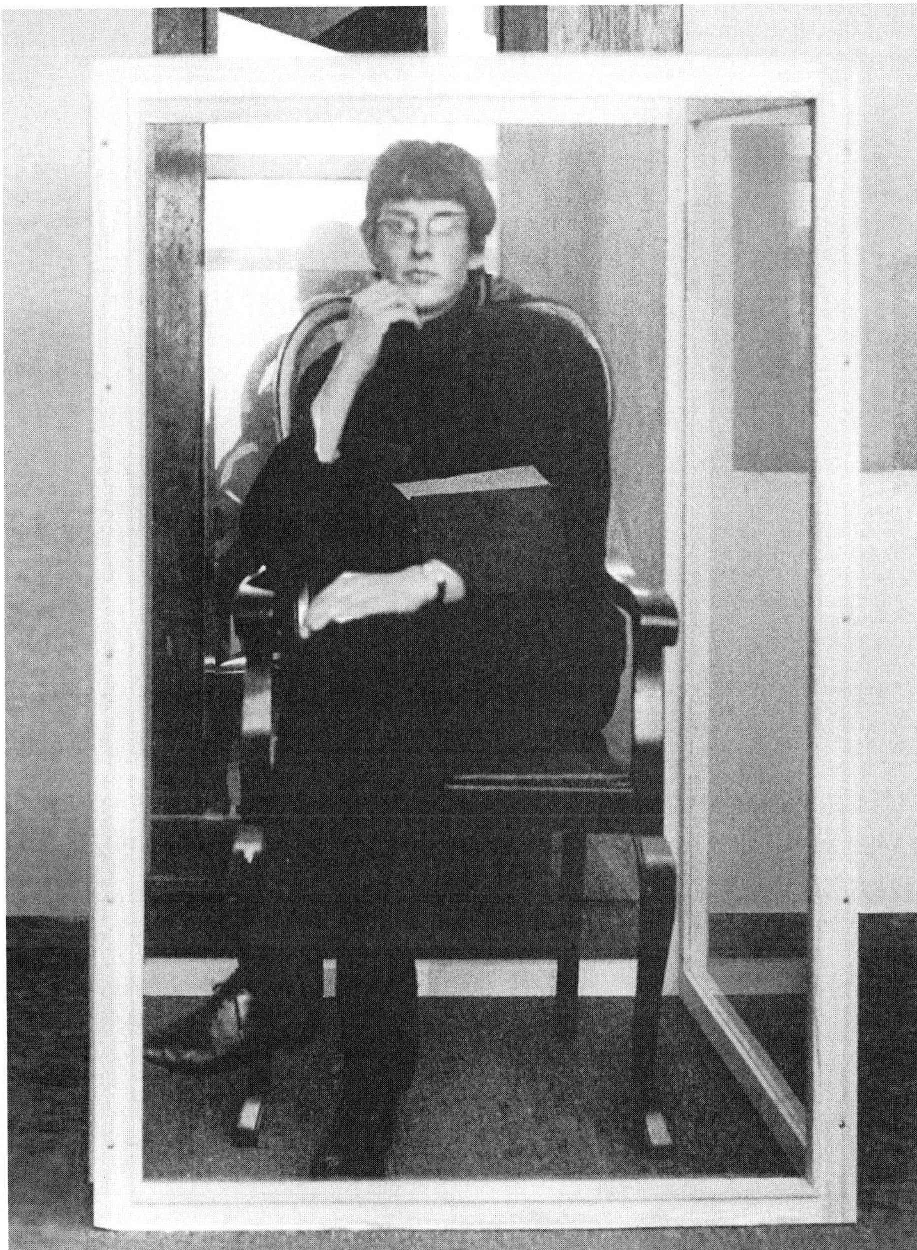

Fig. 3. Timm Ulrichs, *Erstes lebendes Kunstwerk (Selbstausstellung)*, 1965, photography on canvas, 150 x 100 cm. Reproduction from exh. cat. Hannover 2011 (as note 16), 11, fig. 4.

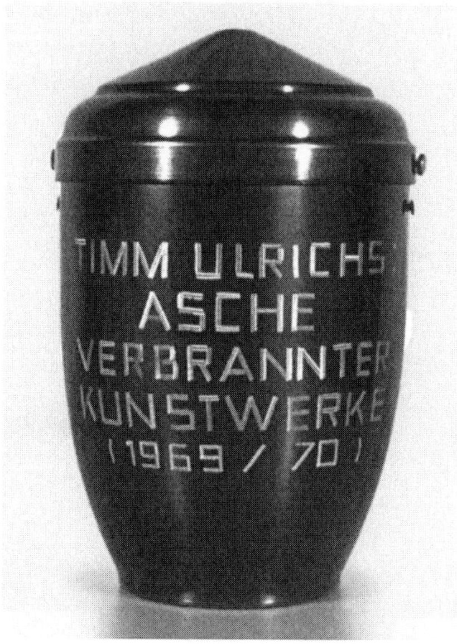

Fig. 4. Timm Ulrichs, *Asche verbrannter Kunstwerke (Kunst-Urne)*, 1969/70. Reproduction from exh. cat. Hannover 2011 (as note 16), 99, fig. 71. © VG Bild-Kunst, Bonn 2014.

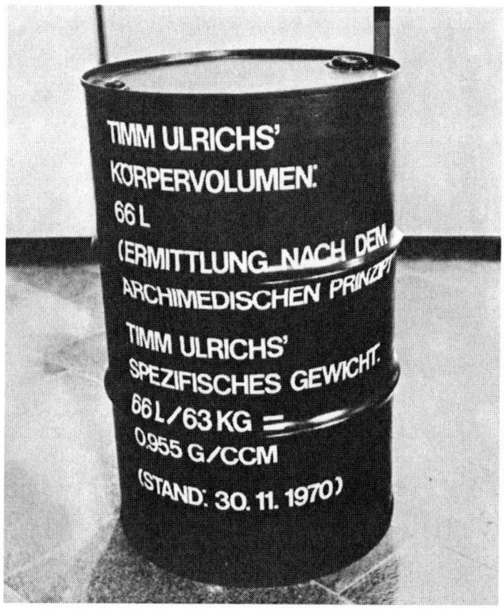

Fig. 5. Timm Ulrichs, *Timm Ulrichs' Körpervolumen und Spezifisches Gewicht (Ermittlung nach dem Archimedischen Prinzip)*, 1970. Reproduction from exh. cat. Braunschweig 1975 (as note 16), 20, fig. 12. © VG Bild-Kunst, Bonn 2014.

of everyday concerns.[14] In one of his collages where he used snippets of newspapers, he accidentally found the word "Merz" as a part of the word "Kommerz"; following this, he called his later works Merz Art ("Merzkunst").[15] In doing so, he made a *motto* out of this word and developed a theory which proclaimed and merchandized this title.

Very important in the art works of the 1960s are the more amusing components. An example would be the self-consciousness of the artist not to take

14 The object is not preserved. Photograph in: Hanne Bergius, *Das Lachen Dadas. Die Berliner Dadaisten und ihre Aktionen* (Werkbund Archiv, vol. 17), Gießen 1993, 293.

15 See Isabel Schulz, "'Was wäre das Leben ohne Merz?' Zur Entwicklung und Bedeutung des Kunstbegriffs von Kurt Schwitters", in: *Aller Anfang ist Merz – Von Kurt Schwitters bis heute*, exh. cat. Sprengel Museum Hannover et al., eds. Susanne Meyer-Büser and Karin Orchard, Stuttgart 2000, 244–251.

himself and his art too seriously, but at the same time his play with words and images to entertain in a moralistic way, which relates to the function of the traditional emblem with its narrative, entertaining or enjoyable character. This purpose of art establishes a direct link to emblems.

*

Another topic beside politics and social-criticism has become more influential to the contemporary art of the 1960s: the question of the relationship between art and everyday-life. The artist Timm Ulrichs, who became famous for his poetic artworks in the 1960s, shows a different way of working with icons and words. Like Alvermann he worked with the ironic break, but in his case – unlike Alvermann – not in a sarcastic, sometimes annoying way, but in an ironic, poetic and transforming game.
Timm Ulrichs was born in Berlin in 1940. He lives in Hannover and taught at the Kunstakademie Münster (Westfalia).[16] His artistic career started with the foundation of an *Advertising-Agency for Total-art and Banalism and Extemporism* in 1961. He pushed the first protests against his art when he decided to exhibit himself in an art exhibition as the first living artwork (fig. 3).[17] The senate of the exhibition promptly changed the guidelines and prohibited works, which cannot be the subject of a legal transaction. Even if his self-exhibition was prohibited, the press took great notice of Ulrich. He included the provocative event-effect and the publicity it caused for his art-concept from the very beginning. In the following, he worked with poetic transformations such as in his work *to name = to mean* in which it becomes obvious that words instead of images take the decisive role in his art.[18]
With symbolizations like *The complete literary oeuvre,* he created a haptic

16 For the biography of Timm Ulrichs see *Timm Ulrichs. Retrospektive 1960-1975,* exh. cat. Kunstverein Braunschweig et al., ed. Heinz Holtmann, Braunschweig 1975, 101. – *Timm Ulrichs. Betreten der Ausstellung verboten! Werke von 1960 bis 2010 / Keep Out of the Exhibition! Works from 1960 to 2010,* exh. cat. Sprengel Museum Hannover and Kunstverein Hannover, eds. Ute Stuffer and René Zechlin, Ostfildern 2011, 209.

17 See Korte-Beuckers 1999 (as note 10), 111–126.

18 See exh. cat. Braunschweig 1975 (as note 16), cat. nr. 39, photo p. 36.

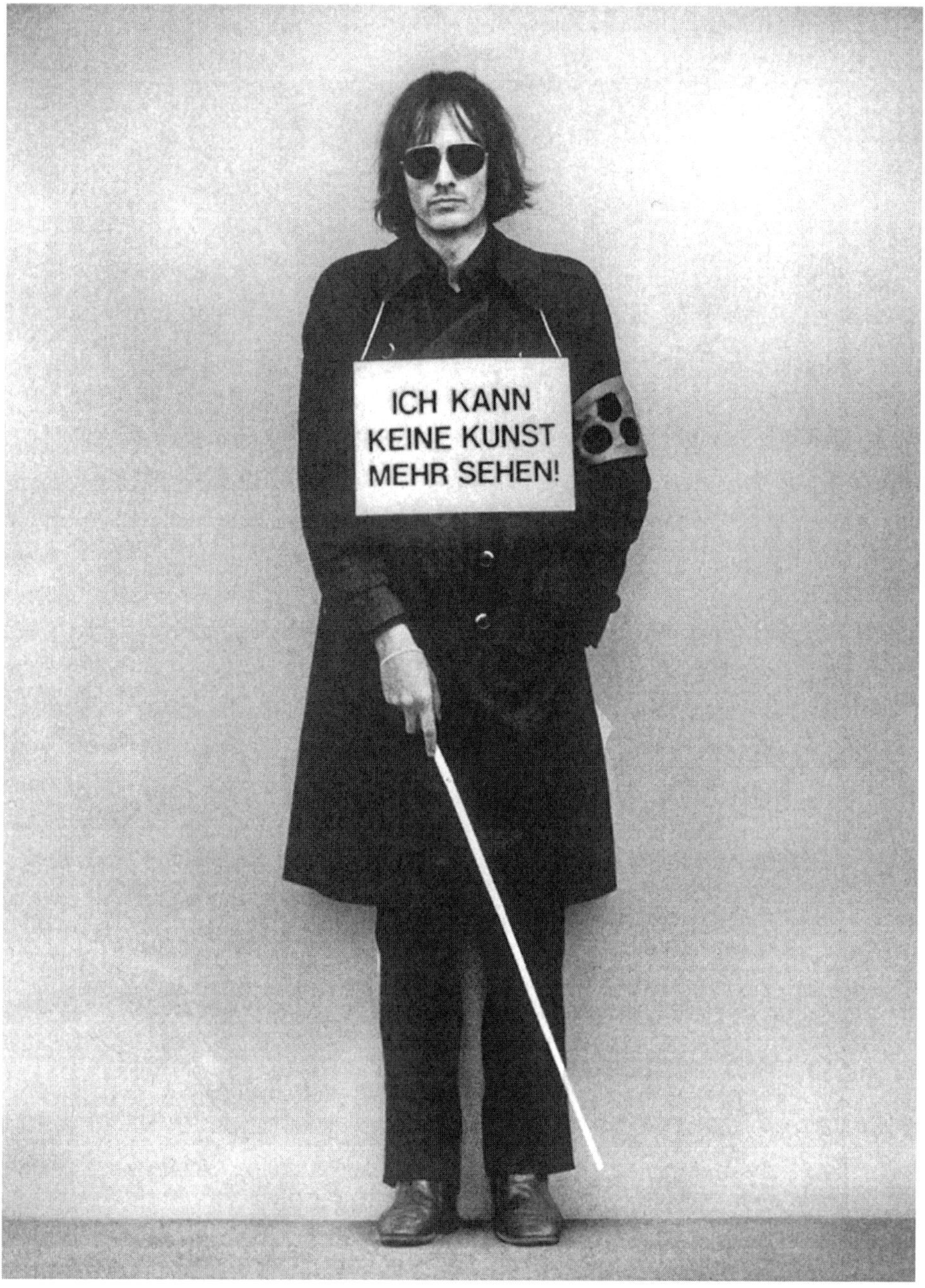

Fig. 6. Timm Ulrichs, *Ich kann keine Kunst mehr sehen*, 1975, photography on canvas, 125 x 100 cm. Reproduction from exh. cat. Hannover 2011 (as note 16), 69, fig. 45 (Photo: Ellen Poerschke). © VG Bild-Kunst, Bonn 2014.

presence of abstract terms with the form of a typewriter ribbon.[19] In questions of emblematic definitions, works like the *Literarisches Gesamtwerk* in 1968 or *Timm Ulrichs ashes: burned pieces of art 1969/70* (fig. 4) give short descriptions on which the objects as icons rely on.[20] Here, however, the words do not refer back to the visualization in a direct or obvious way, but in a double sense of words like in anagrams or in other contexts. In this way, they are as concrete as they are vague and they are as correct as they are non-valid so that the images do not visualize the meaning, but change or question it. According to the construction of emblems, there seems to be a lack of the third part in the form of a *subscriptio* to give further explanations. Within the work of Timm Ulrichs, these explanations are not given within the single piece of art, but they are explicitly explained in dependence on the whole oeuvre which has to be regarded as a unity. Each piece of Ulrichs's art work is in itself part of a more comprehensive unit of the art work, finally making up the artist's whole oeuvre.

By this means, several other artworks give a form of explanation to each single piece of art, beginning with the foundation of the *Werbezentrale für Gesamtkunst* as well as in written explanations and statements like *Timm Ulrichs: Ich als Kunstfigur, oder: was das ganze Theater soll* in his *2. Egozentrisches Manifest.*[21] In case of Timm Ulrichs, the artist himself reaches into the center of his art as a leitmotif. The measures or volume of his body become visualized imaginations as an art-concept in concept-art (fig. 5). In works like *body-volume and specific weight* the observer is even supplied with written information such as a list of contents of the artwork, which additionally aims to explain the principles and results of the artwork.[22]

Further information is given beyond the single piece of art itself. This principle leads to the question of how far single artworks debate or show their meaning without losing part of their significance. For Ulrichs it leads to the result visualized in the artwork *Ich kann keine Kunst mehr sehen* (fig. 6) which

19 See exh. cat. Braunschweig 1975 (as note 16), cat. nr. 40, photo p. 37.
20 See exh. cat. Hannover 2011 (as note 16), cat. nr. 71, photo p. 99.
21 See exh. cat. Braunschweig 1975 (as note 16), 17.
22 See exh. cat. Braunschweig 1975 (as note 16), cat. nr. 12, photo p. 20.

could either be translated as "I cannot see any art anymore" or as "I cannot stand art any longer". In the former case, there is literally no art left to be seen, visualized by the blindness of the artist which is symbolized by his blind stick and armband. So either the artist as an observer is too blind to see art or there is nothing to see anymore.[23] This ambivalence intentionally demonstrates the limits of modern art which as a conceptual idea does not visualize anything anymore or can hardly be distinguished from commodities of everyday life. As soon as all divisions are renounced, for the emblem it could mean that someone has to find the parts of the three-part structure of *lemma, icon* and *epigram* as titles, images and explanations not conjoined in one image and in one time anymore, but with the extension of dimensions divided and parted, and lost within a vast structure of spreading contexts. Therefore, the idea of an *erweiterter Kunstbegriff*, that is to say, an expanded definition of art, which has been on the rise since the 1960s, leads to a wider emblematic definition of contemporary art.

*

Another concept seems to be appropriate concerning the presence of emblematic structures in the art of the 1960s. It is a piece of art by Joseph Kosuth.[24] Kosuth was born 1945 in Toledo, Ohio USA. Since 1967 he was professor of Visual Arts in New York and since 1988 in Germany (Hamburg, Stuttgart, Munich). One of his most prominent and often quoted artworks is *One and Three Chairs* of 1965, which is not only a unique artwork, but also an idea of artwork realized in several varying types.[25] Representing one of the most important topics for his work, it deals with the role of visual im-

23 See exh. cat. Hannover 2011 (as note 16), cat. nr. 45, photo p. 69.

24 For the artistic work of Joseph Kosuth see *Joseph Kosuth. Art Investigations & 'Problematics' since 1965*, exh. cat. Kunstmuseum Luzern, 5 vol., Zürich 1973. – *Joseph Kosuth. Beiträge zur konzeptionellen Kunst 1965 bis 1976*, exh. cat. Kunsthalle Bremen, eds. Friedrich Selchert, Bernhard Schnackenburg and Günter Busch, Bremen 1976. – *Joseph Kosuth. The Making of Meaning. Selected writings and documentation of investigations of art since 1965*, exh. cat. Staatsgalerie Stuttgart et al., ed. Gudrun Inboden, Stuttgart 1981. – *Joseph Kosuth. Kein Ding, Kein Ich, Keine Form, Kein Grundsatz (Sind Sicher) / No Thing, No Self, No Form, No Principle (Was Certain)*, exh. cat. Villa Merkel Esslingen, ed. Reante Damsch-Wiehager, Stuttgart 1993.

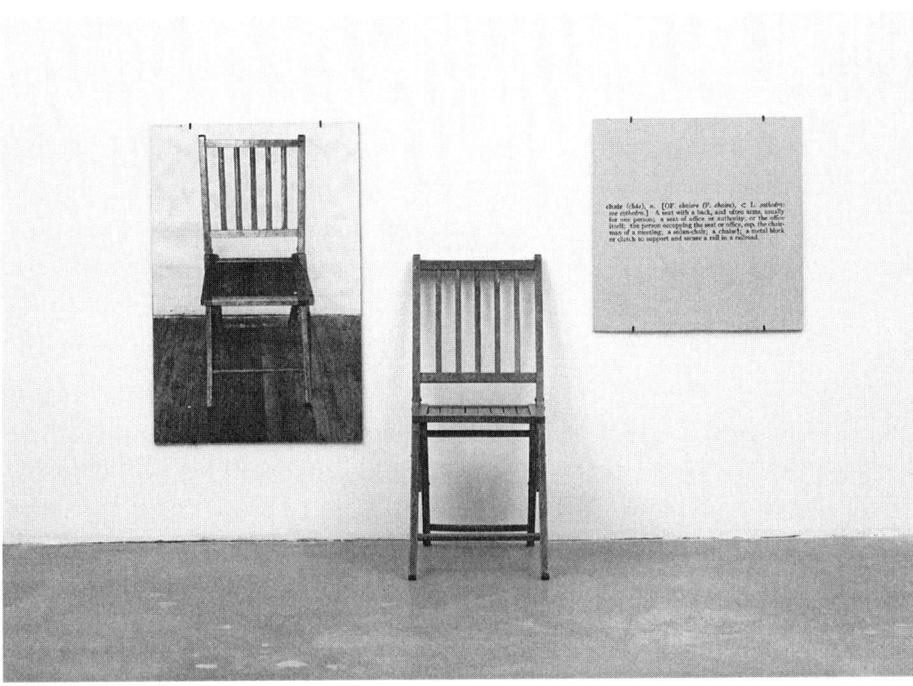

Fig. 7. Joseph Kosuth, *One and Three Chairs,* 1965. © VG Bild-Kunst, Bonn 2014. Photo: Wikiart. Visual Art Encyclopedia.

ages. His analytic way of conceiving Concept Art is dominated by a sensual approach to reality, identity and the essence of being. Kosuth followed the idea that the specific form art would take has to be seen as language to some extent, so that every piece of art, as a *proposition* within its space, would be a commentary on art.[26]

One and Three Chairs shows a common chair placed next to a life-sized photograph of the same chair as well as a blow-up of a copy of a dictionary definition which designates what the term 'chair' is said to mean (fig. 7). This tripartite structure is comparable to an emblematic structure: the chair, the

25 For example, see exh. cat. Bremen 1976 (as note 24), cat. nr. 1 and exh. cat. Dortmund 1989 (as note 13), 41.

26 See Benjamin H.D. Buchloh, "Von der Ästhetik der Verwaltung zur institutionellen Kritik. Einige Aspekte der Konzeptkunst von 1962–1969", in: Exh. cat. Düsseldorf 1990 (as note 5), 86-99, here 91.

photography as a sign for a chair and the explanation given by the dictionary entry. In this work, three different implementations or meanings of one term are shown.

But what leads away from this emblematic idea is that the meaningful whole, that what it is all about, is in this piece of art neither shown in the object or the photograph, nor in the definition or in the title. The meaning of Kosuth's work does not lie in chairs in the first place. Maybe there is a reason for choosing specific items, for example, in the understanding of a chair being an old cultural implement. Yet, it seems rather arbitrarily chosen as an optional example to visualize an abstract idea in opposition to the showing of a concrete commodity. So, the topic of this work deals with questions of identity and fundamental ideas, meanings and the possibility of their visualization. In fact, there are several other objects being presented in the same way, as for example *One and Three ... Shelves, Patterns, Tables, Saws, Hammers, Boxes, Brooms,* just to name a few.[27] According to Charles K. Ogden and Ivor A. Richards, the semiotic triangle consists of three parts: symbol (term), referent (the thing itself) and reference (meaning), which relate to each other in order to create content out of relation.[28] Ferdinand de Saussure emphasized the importance of the difference between signifier and signified, the difference between the signs and the referent,[29] and it is obvious that Kosuth deals with these concepts of epitomes of meaning. In his work he often makes reference to the term of investigation as a principle of art referring to

27 For example, see exh. cat. Luzern 1973 (as note 24), cat. nr. 14–16, 27 and 29 and exh. cat. Bremen 1976 (as note 24), cat. nr. 2 and 3.

28 Charles K. Ogden and Ivor A. Richards, *The Meaning of Meaning. A Study of the Influence of Language upon Thought and of the Science of Symbolism*, San Diego 1989 [first published 1923]. – See also Caroline Boller, *'Das Problem der Bedeutung' nach C. V. Ogden und I. A. Richards im Zusammenhang mit Franz Boas' Auffassung von Sprache*, Munich 2008. – Mathias Haller, *Die Beziehung zwischen Bedeutung, Bezugsgegenstand, Übersetzung und Gebrauch. Sprachphilosophie des 20. Jahrhunderts*, Munich 2012.

29 Ferdinand de Saussure, *Cours de linguistique générale*, Paris 1922, German edition ed. by Peter Wunderli, Tübingen 2014. – See Ludwig Jäger, *Ferdinand de Saussure. Zur Einführung*, Hamburg 2010.

30 See *Art & Language (M. Baldwin, T. Atkinson, P. Pilkington, D. Rushton)*, in: Exh. cat. Luzern 1973 (as note 24), vol. 1, 30. – Paul Maenz and Gerd de Vries: "Joseph Kosuth: 'Kunst existiert nur in Form von Praxis'", in: Exh. cat. Bremen 1976 (as note 24).

itself in a tautological way. To sum up, the meaning of his work is not about the objects being shown or described, but about the ways in which they are shown in terms of visualization as a kind of reflexive item, hinting at nothing else but itself.[30]

*

Within contemporary art with its expanded definition of art and a scientific approach to meaning and definition, it could be asked whether exact parallel emblematic structures can be discerned, and, with regard to an expanded definition of art, whether an expanded definition of what constitutes an emblematic structure is desirable as well and where it might eventually lead. Wherever pieces of art are titled in a way transcending a mere numbering or a descriptive title, a second dimension of meaning as the motto of the icon-structure is opened. Its sense or meaning is based on an extended topic of written or shown signs, relating to individual experiences or a collective consciousness. Following Jacques Derrida, it seems possible to spread this topic "in a manner which is absolutely illimitable"[31] because the combination of signs can extend, and thereby alter and vary every given context.
In today's art, there are many different attempts to deal with the combination of visions, imaginations, inscriptions and explanations. For example, there is an art work by the Welsh artist Cerith Wyn Evans (born in 1958) called *In girum imus nocte et consumimur igni,*[32] created in 1997 which is a palindromic Latin phrase translating into "We go round and round at night and are consumed by fire". At the same time, this is the title of a film by Guy

31 Jacques Derrida, "Signature Event Context" [1971], in: Jacques Derrida, *Limited Inc.*, Evanston 1988, 1–24, here 12: "Every sign, linguistic or nonlinguistic, spoken or written (in the current sense of this opposition), in a small or large unit, can be *cited,* put between quotation marks; in so doing it can break with every given context, engendering an infinity of new contexts in a manner which is absolutely illimitable." http://www.clas.ufl.edu/users/burt/inc.pdf (accessed 10 September 2014).

32 See *Cerith Wyn Evans... Visibleinvisible,* exh. cat. MUSAC. Museo de Arte Contemporáneo de Castilla y León, ed. Octavio Zaya, Ostfildern 2008, 87.

Debord. With the illumination of the neon-letters, Wyn Evans symbolically visualizes the meaning of his work and the active role that the audience has to take: by circumambulating the work, he causes equivalences in text and action in a kind of self-referring adaption process.[33] The way the words are set in an illuminated neon-writing in a round form evokes associations of a chandelier. Hence, it is the individual impression, imagination and the behavior of the spectators which visualize the wider spread of meaning, combined also with the historic reference of the words quoting Guy Debord's film. The Latin phrase might as well be comparable to the integration of classical Latin text often inherent in the composition of emblems.

Within the last years, various artists took up the idea of a combination of image and motto. As an example, the artworks of the German artist Julius von Bismarck (born in 1983) deal with this tradition. In his *No-projection* about Pope John Paul II. (Pope 1978–2005) from 1994 he projected words on people's photos.[34] Von Bismarck developed a so-called image fulgurator, comparable to a camera with a flashlight which will be triggered by other flashlights, subsequently projecting words on other people's photos that cannot be seen in the real event of taking a photo. It causes invasive manipulations of photography. In this way, von Bismarck not only philosophically picks up on questions from possible different spheres of reality but also gives political statements.

Both contemporary art concepts deal with these ideas of *lemma, icon* and *epigram* in a new way. This demonstrates the ongoing lasting meaning of these emblem-like structures in today's art. Since the extension of the definition of art in the 1960s, concepts have changed faster than theories do. This is why for the future there will have to be a flexible concept of the definition of emblematic structures able to take into consideration all the

33 See Hanna Pahl, *Zum Werk von Cerith Wyn Evans*, typoscript Magisterarbeit University of Kiel 2010, 10.

34 See Julius von Bismarck, Image Fulgurator. http://juliusvonbismarck.com/bank/index.php?/projects/fulgurator-tech/ (accessed 10 September 2014).

35 See Klaus Gereon Beuckers, "Vorwort", in: *Architektur als Ort für Embleme. Beiträge zu einer Tagung des Kunsthistorischen Instituts der Christian-Albrechts-Universität zu Kiel am 26.01.2013* (Mundus Symbolicus, vol. 2), ed. Ingrid Höpel, Kiel 2014, 7–8, here 7.

36 Exh. cat. Esslingen 1992 (as note 24), cover.

different usages of the manifold ideas effecting the combination of words and pictures.

*

Concerning today's art, it seems less important to look at emblematic art in a traditional way, because this seems to lead to eclecticisms and historical resources in unfitting artistic devices. The question of emblematic structures could rather pave the way for structural analysis, in which the division of the specific form of presentation, of function and meaning, could form a pattern for the approach to questions concerning art-concepts dealing with a combination of words and images and with the common crossover of art and literature. As the history of emblematic researches shows, a change in theoretical ways – approaching the topic from divergent definitions of what the central aspect of emblems was meant to be, whether a kind of symbol, allegory or ideogram in a more visual or rather theoretical, mental or notional kind,[35] – opens up a widespread topic concerning the intersection of pictures and words.

Robert Musil's remarks about Kosuth remind us not to strictly adhere to traditional forms, but to vary and accommodate concepts so that they can remain adequate for today's circumstances: "[Kosuth] sensed that this order was not so firm as it presented to be; no thing, no self, no form, no principle was certain. Everything is caught up in invisible but never-resting metamorphosis; in the unfirm lies more of the future than the firm, and the present is nothing but a hypothesis which one has not yet gotten beyond."[36]

Behind the Comforting Facades. On Taryn Simon's *An American Index of the Hidden and Unfamiliar* (2007) as a Contemporary Emblem Book

Susanne Schwertfeger

Over a period of four years, Taryn Simon has visited places and organizations which had not been visible to the public eye up to that point – some of them we might not even have thought would exist.[1] The spectrum ranges from such institutions as the Lucasfilm Archives, where, among other things, the props from the STARWARS Movies are preserved, to the Imperial Office of the Ku Klux Klan. Also included are the Nonlinear Dynamics Laboratory in Maryland, where an artificial Earth core generates a self-sustaining magnetic field, and the so called 'Body Farm', where human corpses are decomposing in an open site in order to gain forensic data. The permission for Simon to enter these areas – usually closed to any kind of private access – was the result of an intensive and long-winded communication process.

*

The photographs she brought from those visits are compiled in *An American Index of the Hidden and Unfamiliar* (2007),[2] with each picture accompanied

1 Taryn Simon consciously started her artistic research and work as a reaction to the efforts of the American Government to search for hidden places outside the borders of the U.S.A., particularly in the context of the Iraq War, where photographs and their 'reading' were used as a legitimization for military actions. See Kay von Rabenau, "Taryn Simon: Kaleidoscope of Entropy", in: *Mono Kultur* 15 (December 2007/January 2008), 4.

2 Taryn Simon, *An American Index of the Hidden and Unfamiliar*, 2nd ed., Göttingen 2008, 19.

by a text per spread.[3] We can identify alternating main themes or categories such as religion, politics, nature, culture/art, and science, which mutually penetrate and overlap with each other. They are intentionally not put into a particular order, nor are they clustered, because "[t]he work is meant to be disorienting."[4] Nevertheless, along with the formation into a fixed sequence due to the medium of the book,[5] comes an opening and a closing image. Both are able to set a certain tone on how to approach the images in between. For the *American Index* Taryn Simon chose the picture of a nuclear waste facility (fig. 1), which merges the concept of the project on various levels: not only is the view into a holding basin with capsules of nuclear waste rather uncommon, but the glowing blue aura furthermore visualizes the otherwise 'hidden'/invisible radiation.

At first glance, the term 'unfamiliar' at first glance seems to address related aspects: something that is not frequently seen, heard or experienced, and on that note is 'hidden' from our knowledge and the possibility of acquaintance. But the 'unfamiliar' is also a basic part of the concept of the 'uncanny', and though

> we are tempted to conclude that what is 'uncanny' is frightening precisely because it is *not* known and familiar [...] this uncanny is in reality nothing new or alien, but something which is familiar and old-established in the mind and which has become alienated from it only through the process of repression. This reference to the factor of repression enables us, furthermore, to understand Schelling's definition of the uncanny as something which ought to have remained hidden but has come to light.[6]

This content correlation, which Freud calls the "secret nature of the uncanny",[7] still echoes in the German pairing of the meanwhile outdated 'das Heimelige'/'das Heimliche' (for 'familiar' or 'homely') and 'das Unheimliche' (for 'uncanny' – or literally: 'unfamiliar').

The aspect of the uncanny is implicit in Simon's photos and it sneaks in quietly through the perceptual process of cognition, when something apparently familiar is loaded with a new, sinister meaning, or a well-known image emerges from unexpected and uneasy circumstances – as for example randomized capsules of a nuclear waste facility, with their deathly glow of radiation, forming the trusted outlines of the United States of America. This

eerie map can be seen as a reference to the utilization of the American flag in Robert Frank's *The Americans* (1958),[8] in which it appears prominently at the beginning of each of the four sections of the photobook. So both Frank and Simon start their work with "a symbol of obvious national significance and graphic strength".[9] Frank's intention was an "observation and a record of what one naturalized American finds to see in the United States that signifies the kind of civilization born here and spreading elsewhere."[10]
Taryn Simon's *American Index,* however, questions what nowadays can't be *found* or *seen* "by one citizen", because of the division "between expert and public access and knowledge"[11] (which also implies an intentional act of hiding). It also unfolds what is gladly forgotten while it is *spreading inside* the American nation and culture.

*

3 Seven out of the 58 topics received a photograph and a text on both sides of the spread: the CIA Original Headquarter Building (42/43), the Lucasfilm Archives (36/37), the Cryonics Institute (66/67), the Deliberation Room of DOAR Litigation Consulting (84/85), the Cheyenne Mountain Directorate (92, 93), the Military Operation on Urban Terrain in Fort Campbell (102/103), and the Plum Island Animal Disease Center (114/115). Simon 2008 (as note 2).

4 David Coggins, "Taryn Simon", in: *Interview magazine* [29. November 2008], http://www.interviewmagazine.com/art/taryn-simon/# (accessed 26 August 2014).

5 At the same time with the publication of the book, the work has also been presented as chromogenic prints (94,6 x 113 cm; edition of 7) at The Withney Museum of American Art (2007) and at the Museum für Moderne Kunst, Frankfurt am Main (2007/2008). Nonetheless the museum presentations, Simon always turns her finished projects into a book which can stand alone. In case of *The American Index* she wanted to assures the connection between the two elements and their vice versa transformation, for "[i]n exhibitions, the viewer initially engages with the work as an aesthetic object". Coggins 2008 (as note 4).

6 Sigmund Freud, "The *Uncanny*", first published in: *Imago. Zeitschrift für Anwendung der Psychoanalyse auf die Geisteswissenschaften,* vol. V (1919), quoted in: http://web.mit.edu/allanmc/www/freud1.pdf [trans. Alix Strachey] (accessed 26 August 2014).

7 Freud 1919 (as note 6).

8 Robert Frank, *The Americans,* New York 1959 [first published as: Robert Frank, *Les Américans,* Paris 1958].

9 *Looking in Robert Frank's The Americans,* exh. cat. National Gallery of Art Washington, ed. Sarah Greenough, Göttingen 2009, 177.

10 Exh. cat. Washington 2009 (as note 9), 209.

11 Coggins 2008 (as note 4).

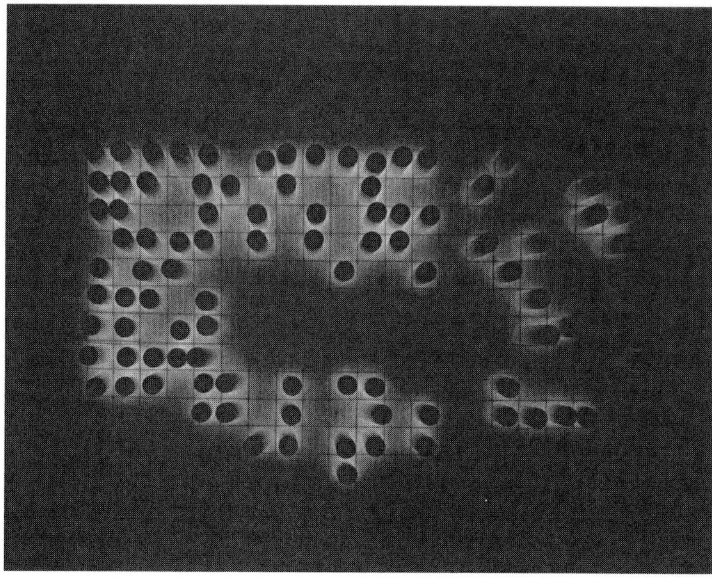

Nuclear Waste Encapsulation and Storage Facility, Cherenkov Radiation
Hanford Site, U.S. Department of Energy
Southeastern Washington State

Submerged in a pool of water at Hanford Site are 1,936 stainless steel nuclear waste capsules containing cesium and strontium. Combined, they contain over 120 million curies of radioactivity. It is estimated to be the most curies under one roof in the United States. The blue glow is created by the Cherenkov Effect or Cherenkov radiation. The Cherenkov Effect describes the electromagnetic radiation emitted when a charged particle, giving off energy, moves faster than light through a transparent medium. The temperatures of the capsules are as high as 330 degrees Fahrenheit. The pool of water serves as a shield against radiation; a human standing one foot from an unshielded capsule would receive a lethal dose of radiation in less than ten seconds.

Hanford is a 586 square mile former plutonium production complex. It was built for the Manhattan Project, the U.S.-led World War II defense effort that developed the first nuclear weapons. Hanford plutonium was used in the atomic bomb dropped on Nagasaki in 1945. For decades afterwards Hanford manufactured nuclear materials for use in bombs. At Hanford there are more than 53 million gallons of radioactive and chemically hazardous liquid waste, 2,300 tons of spent nuclear fuel, nearly 18 metric tons of plutonium-bearing materials and about 80 square miles of contaminated groundwater. It is among the most contaminated sites in the United States.

Fig. 1. Taryn Simon, *Nuclear Waste Encapsulation and Storage Facility, Cherenkov Radiation Hanford Site, US Department of Energy Southeastern Washington State*, 2007, photography. Reprod. from Taryn Simon, *An American Index of the Hidden and Unfamiliar*, 2nd ed., Göttingen 2008, p. 19. © Taryn Simon. Courtesy Gagosian Gallery.

The artist therefore does not follow the typical modes of the photobook, in which the pictures are the superior or even only source of information, or accompanied by a continuous text in the manner of 'photo-texts'.[12] She instead adapts a structure which resembles the aesthetics of many emblem books, with each subject given one spread, image and text on the right while the left side is mostly left blank. The page is dominated by the prominently placed image/*pictura* in the upper part, whereas the column of the text/*subcriptio* or *epigram* below is narrower. But above all, Simon more particularly utilizes an emblematic strategy, most notably in both the respective comprehension of its textual and pictorial element and the synergetic effect through a combined and mutual reading of both media, as will be demonstrated in the following.

The content of the paragraphs as the textual element goes far beyond small captions or mere picture-related descriptions. In addition to the photograph of the nuclear waste facility in Hanford, we learn that "[t]he temperatures of the capsules are as high as 330 degrees Fahrenheit. The pool of water serves as a shield against radiation; a human standing one foot from an unshielded capsule would receive a lethal dose of radiation in less than ten seconds."[13]

Beside listing what can be seen, all *epigrams* contain statistical data and notable as well as unexpected and rather disturbing facts and connections, revealing what is (still) unseen: "[Hanford] was built for the Manhattan Project" and that "Hanford plutonium was used in the atomic bomb dropped on Nagasaki in 1945."[14] Such information in an act of exegesis highlights another quality of the picture: The former somehow mystical and pleasant image of abstract patterns turned into the symbol of a nation, and turns again – but this time into an indexical sign for an invisible potency, the application of which is not restricted to generating energy for everyone's everyday life but has already been utilized as a weapon of mass destruction.

The final passages of every *epigram* open up a wider perspective, in the

12 See Stephen H. Longmire, *Picture a Life: The Photo-texts of Wright Morris*, PhD dissertation, University of Chicago 2010, v-viii.

13 Simon 2008 (as note 2), 19.

14 Simon 2008 (as note 2), 19.

manner of a main point: with "more than 53 million gallons of radioactive and chemically hazardous liquid waste, [the area of Hanford's Nuclear Waste facility is] among the most contaminated sites in the United States".[15] In case of the first page, this final sentence prefigures the "sites" presented on the upcoming pages, and the picture further recalls a warning sign before the reader/viewer enters to the explore the hidden and unfamiliar.

*

Similar to a 'traditional emblem', the pictorial element in Simon's work shows a "changed degree of reality".[16] Though it is the nature of photography that it can only show an abridged 'reality'[17] from the past, the viewer's perception is often the converse. The artist is well aware of the suggestive power of the medium[18] and therefore uses the evident artificial tectonics of the emblem to emphasize its selective character. The obvious arrangement, the choreography of light and color of the photographs never disguise their staged nature and by this imply that the depicted moment is a fragment taken from a whole non-depicted cosmos.[19] Simon at the same time carefully avoids any elements that could refer to the genre of documentary, such as grainy appearance or individuals who seem unconscious of having been photographed. The majority of the portrayed look directly into the camera and at the viewer, such as *Don James, Spokesman for 'Compassion & Choices'* in his wheelchair on page 87 (fig. 2). James' figure is centered in an otherwise empty room, colored in warm brown and ochre hues. The scant light from behind hardly reaches his swollen hands folded in his lap and the support

15 Simon 2008 (as note 2), 19.

16 Albrecht Schöne, *Emblematik und Drama im Zeitalter des Barock*, München 1993, 26.

17 'Reality' is used like "that-has-been" here, in terms of the disposition in Barthes' *Camera Lucida* (1980). This means the camera has captured a scene which occurred in that form in that very moment in front of its lens. See Roland Barthes, *Die helle Kammer. Bemerkungen zur Photographie*, Frankfurt am Main 1980, 87.

18 In Taryn Simon's work *The Innocent* (2003), she documented "the stories of individuals who served time in prison for violent crimes they did not commit. At issue is the question of photography's function as a credible eyewitness and arbiter of justice.", in: http://tarynsimon.com/works_innocents.php (accessed 26 August 2014).

stockings, but it emphasizes the face. He looks at us with a faint smile. His appearance gives the impression that he is of poor health or challenged by age, but judging by the calm expression seems to have come to terms with his status. The *en-face* pose of an older man, looking out of the picture and of course the chiaroscuro treatment of the light, as well as the earthy palette resemble the late self portraits of Rembrandt from the 1660s, especially the *Self Portrait at the Age of 63* (1669; London, National Gallery).[20] In this painting, the artist "while the hint of a smile plays around his lips"[21] presents himself through his at that time antiquated apparel "in the guise of a master from the past",[22] just as Simon's photo presents James in the tradition of the honorable old master portraits. Perry Chapman's remark that "[d]espite his age, [they] still powerfully project inner confidence and self-assurance"[23] applies to Rembrandt's last self portraits and the image of Don James alike. Yet, although the single features of the photograph mentioned above recall Rembrandt, there is a significant exception in the composition of the picture in the *American Index*: The sitting posture – which plays only a minor part in the painting – is emphasized to an enormous spatial extent as well as through the reflections from the wheelchair, which are almost the only element to structure the lower part of the scene. This type of pose can be traced back to throne portraits of rulers, for example of Roman emperors, or papal

19 This process of arranging the setting and taking the pictures herself marks one of the basic differences to another well-known 'photobook', the *Kriegsfibel* by Bertold Brecht. Brecht combined found material with his own text, which works against the original intention of the picture or subscription in order to a reframing-process. These 'photoepigrams', as Brecht titled them, have been the object of emblematic studies, initially by Reinhold Grimm's article *Marxistische Emblematik* (1969). See Reinhold Grimm, "Marxistische Emblematik. Zu Bertolt Brechts *Kriegsfibel*", in: *Wissenschaft als Dialog* [Festschrift für Wolfdietrich Rasch], eds. Renate von Heydebrand and Klaus Günther Just, Stuttgart 1969, 351-379. – Thomas von Steinaecker, *Literarische Foto-Texte: Zur Funktion der Fotografien in den Texten Rolf Dieter Brinkmanns, Alexander Kluges und W.G. Sebalds*, Bielefeld 2007, 75-93.

20 *Rembrandt by himself*, exh. cat. National Gallery London, eds. Christopher White and Quentin Buvelot, Göttingen 1999, no. 84, 223-225.

21 Exh. cat. London 1999 (as note 20), 223.

22 Exh. cat. London 1999 (as note 20), 225.

23 H. Perry Chapman, *Rembrandt's Self-Portraits. A Study in Seventeenth-Century Identity*, New Jersey 1990, 130.

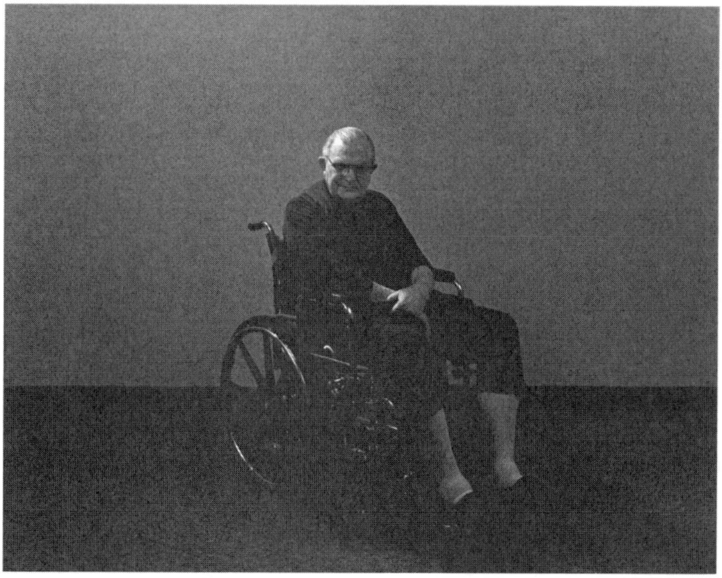

Death with Dignity Act
Don James, former spokesman for *Compassion & Choices*
Portland, Oregon

In 2001 Don James was diagnosed with terminal prostate cancer. At the time of this photograph the cancer had metastasized to the bone. On August 19, 2005, Don exercised his right to receive a prescription for a lethal dose of pentobarbital (Nembutal). He was photographed after filling the prescription. The prescription reads: "Take the entire dose at one time." Don was adamant about the opportunity to have a dignified death and to avoid severe pain. He was supported in his decision by Claire, his wife of 60 years and their four children.

In 1994, Oregon citizens voted to enact the only physician assisted suicide law in the United States. This landmark law, the Death with Dignity Act, permits physicians to prescribe lethal doses of medications for people with terminal illnesses who have less than six months to live. In 2001, former U.S. Attorney General John Ashcroft issued a directive to the federal Drug Enforcement Agency to ban prescription privileges for and criminally prosecute physicians who participated in Oregon's Death with Dignity Act.

Ashcroft's directive was placed on hold during the five years it took advocates of the law to be heard by the U.S. Supreme Court. Don James submitted a declaration to the Supreme Court because he feared he might lose his right to use Oregon's law. In 2006 in the case of *Gonzales v. Oregon*, the Supreme Court ruled in favor of Oregon. Don's life ended without taking the medication, shortly after filling his prescription. From 1998 to 2005, 246 patients have used Oregon's Death with Dignity Act to hasten their deaths.

Fig. 2. Taryn Simon, *Death with Dignity Act Don James, Spokesman for Compassion & Choices Portland, Oregon*, 2007, photography. Reprod. from Taryn Simon, *An American Index of the Hidden and Unfamiliar*, 2nd ed., Göttingen 2008, p. 87. © Taryn Simon. Courtesy Gagosian Gallery.

portraits, with Rafael's *Portrait of Pope Julius II* coming to the fore.[24] Because of the throne Julius is represented as a monarch, claiming not only spiritual but also political power.[25] Furthermore, the thoughtful downward gaze makes him human, almost vulnerable.

Taryn Simon uses this established subgenre of monarch portraits within the portrait category to depict her sitter as empowered and confident. The *epigram* informs us that Don James was diagnosed with terminal prostate cancer in 2001 and claimed the right to end his life under the *Death with Dignity Act* in 2005.[26] This is a landmark law which only exists in two states of the U.S. and allows physicians to prescribe certain patients a lethal dose of pentobarbital. However, to end one's own life – even with the help of physicians (who technically vow to preserve life) – is still a taboo. Thus the *Death with Dignity Act* is frequently questioned and Don James too had to fight to assert his right. The photo was taken on the day he finally filled his prescription. Even if the finitude of life and mortality come to one's mind in observing the picture – the somehow twisted dimension of how exactly death is approached can only be experienced by reading the *epigram*. With this interdependent relationship in mind, Simon takes advantage of an emblematic strategy, as their "tension-stimulating expectation and their surprising solution entails the activation of the recipient."[27]

*

As in the Don James portrait, Taryn Simons uses art historical categories to add recognizable aesthetic implications linked to consensual contents. It is not just art historical influence or repetition of motifs, but a conscious procedure and a selective process in order to denote a certain discourse. Many of the photographs in the *American Index* refer to Dutch or Flemish masterpieces of the 17th century, which was the Golden Age for the arts and espe-

24 There are three known versions of the *Portrait of Pope Julius II* by Raphael, originating ca. 1511/12: National Gallery, London; Uffizi Gallery, Florence; Städel Museum, Frankfurt am Main.

25 At the time of the genesis of the painting, the papacy demanded political right to various lands in Italy.

26 Simon 2008 (as note 2), 87.

27 Steinaecker 2007 (as note 19), 87 [translated by author].

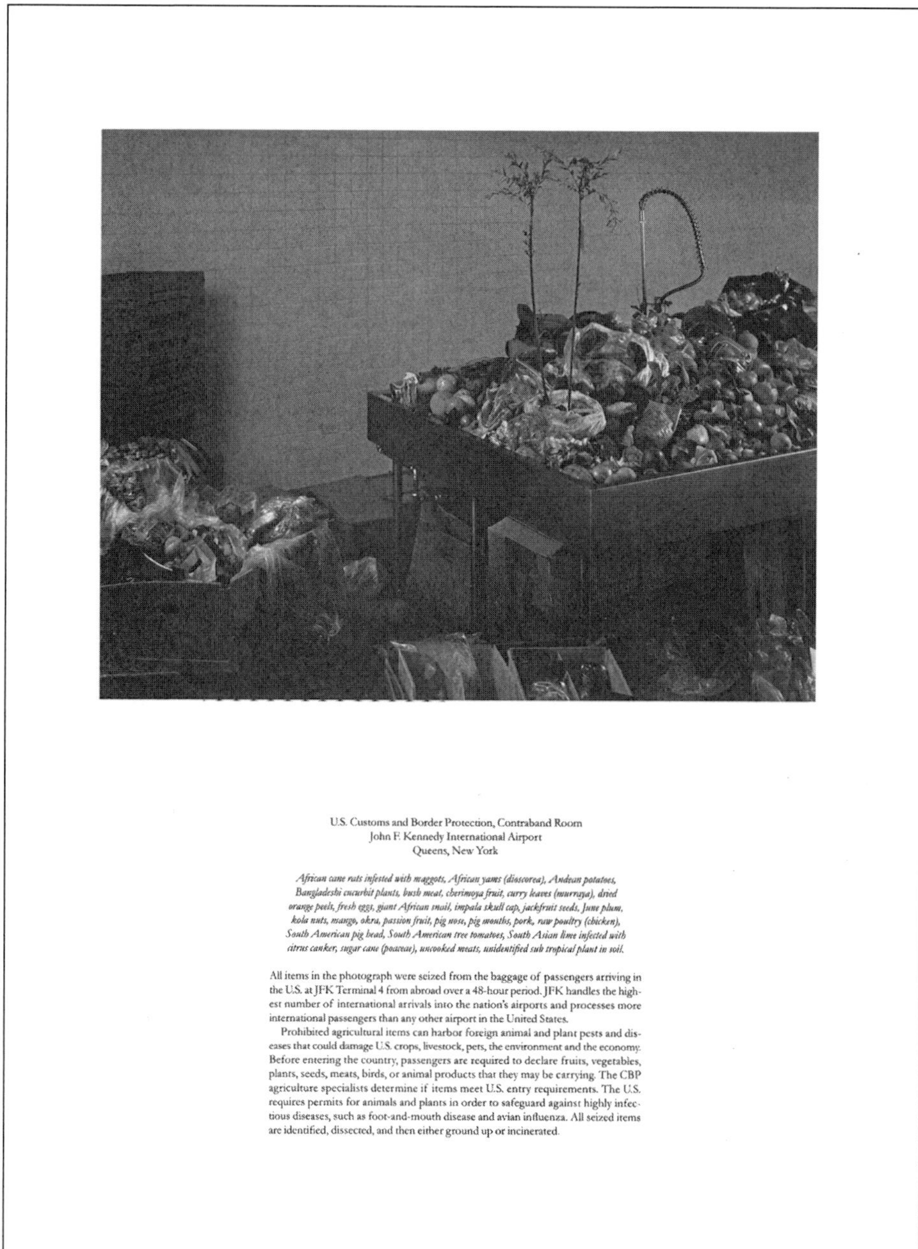

U.S. Customs and Border Protection, Contraband Room
John F. Kennedy International Airport
Queens, New York

African cane rats infested with maggots, African yams (dioscorea), Andean potatoes, Bangladeshi cucurbit plants, bush meat, cherimoya fruit, curry leaves (murraya), dried orange peels, fresh eggs, giant African snail, impala skull cap, jackfruit seeds, June plum, kola nuts, mango, okra, passion fruit, pig nose, pig mouths, pork, raw poultry (chicken), South American pig head, South American tree tomatoes, South Asian lime infected with citrus canker, sugar cane (poaceae), uncooked meats, unidentified sub tropical plant in soil.

All items in the photograph were seized from the baggage of passengers arriving in the U.S. at JFK Terminal 4 from abroad over a 48-hour period. JFK handles the highest number of international arrivals into the nation's airports and processes more international passengers than any other airport in the United States.

Prohibited agricultural items can harbor foreign animal and plant pests and diseases that could damage U.S. crops, livestock, pets, the environment and the economy. Before entering the country, passengers are required to declare fruits, vegetables, plants, seeds, meats, birds, or animal products that they may be carrying. The CBP agriculture specialists determine if items meet U.S. entry requirements. The U.S. requires permits for animals and plants in order to safeguard against highly infectious diseases, such as foot-and-mouth disease and avian influenza. All seized items are identified, dissected, and then either ground up or incinerated.

Fig. 3. Taryn Simon, *U.S. Customs and Border Protection, Contraband Room, John F. Kennedy International Airport, Queens, New York*, 2007, photography. Reprod. from Taryn Simon, *An American Index of the Hidden and Unfamiliar*, 2nd ed., Göttingen 2008, p. 75. © Taryn Simon. Courtesy Gagosian Gallery.

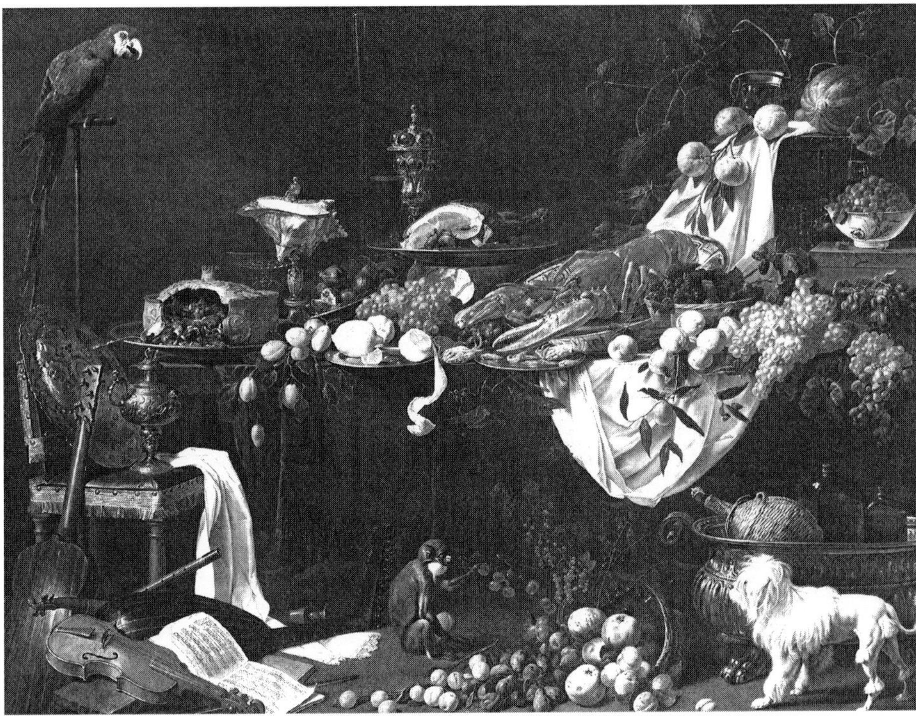

Fig. 4. Adrian van Utrecht, *Magnificent Still Life*, 1644, oil on canvas, 185 x 242.5 cm. Rijksmuseum Amsterdam. Photo: Rijksmuseum Amsterdam.

cially for emblematics. In *U.S. Customs and Border Protection, Contraband Room* (fig. 3)[28] the baroque still-life scheme, once representing the pride of luxury goods imported from the colonies (fig. 4), is turned into a display of rotting groceries, confiscated by the border Protection at the Kennedy Airport in fear of contagious diseases. We also find compositions in color or structure that draw connections between contemporary American culture and milestones of American art, for example Marc Rothko (p. 131) or Jackson Pollock (p. 81).

Another important American aesthetic references are the plates of John James Audubon. He was the most influential ornithologist and author, as well as artist, of *Birds of America* (1827-38), which occasionally ranked as

28 Simon 2008 (as note 2), 75.

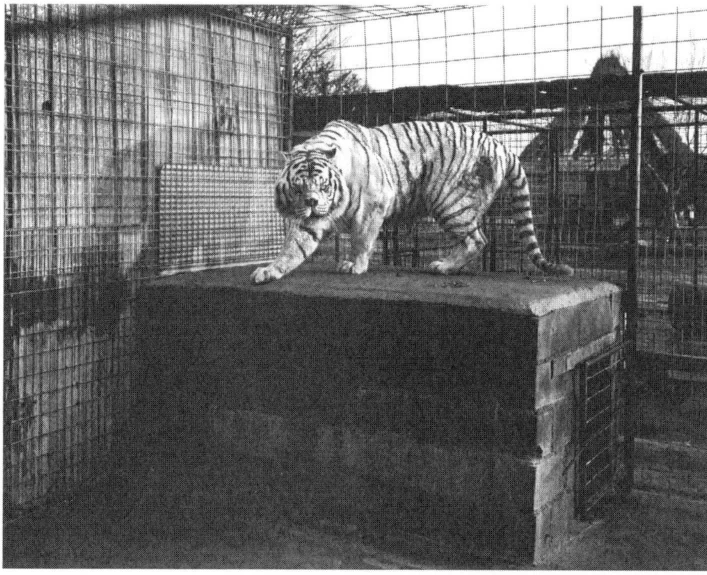

White Tiger (Kenny), Selective Inbreeding
Turpentine Creek Wildlife Refuge and Foundation
Eureka Springs, Arkansas

Kenny was born to a breeder in Bentonville, Arkansas on February 3, 1999. As a result of inbreeding, Kenny has mental retardation and significant physical limitations. Due to his deep-set nose, he has difficulty breathing and closing his jaw, his teeth are severely malformed and he limps from abnormal bone structure in his forearms.

White tigers are extremely rare in their natural habitats in Asia. In the U.S., all living white tigers are the result of selective inbreeding in captivity to artificially create the genetic conditions that lead to white fur, ice-blue eyes and a pink nose. Currently, inbreeding such as father to daughter, brother to sister, mother to son has become commonplace. It produces a white cub less than 25% of the time, with only approximately 3% of those considered "quality." The three other tigers in Kenny's litter are not considered to be quality white tigers as they are yellow coated, cross-eyed, and knock-kneed.

Conservation experts challenge the perception that white tigers are a rare and endangered species. Instead, they state that zoos, breeders, and entertainment acts have over-bred white tigers for financial gain, citing instances where private breeders and zoos have sold "quality" white tigers for over $60,000. The grave health consequences of inbreeding and over-breeding have led to abortions, stillbirths and a high mortality rate among infants. The Species Survival Plan has condemned the practice. In recent years there has been a significant drop in their market value.

Fig. 5. Taryn Simon, *White Tiger (Kenny), Selective Inbreeding, Turpentine Creek Wildlife Refuge and Foundation, Eureka Springs, Arkansas*, 2007, photography. Reprod. from Taryn Simon, *An American Index of the Hidden and Unfamiliar*, 2nd ed., Göttingen 2008, p. 55. © Taryn Simon. Courtesy Gagosian Gallery.

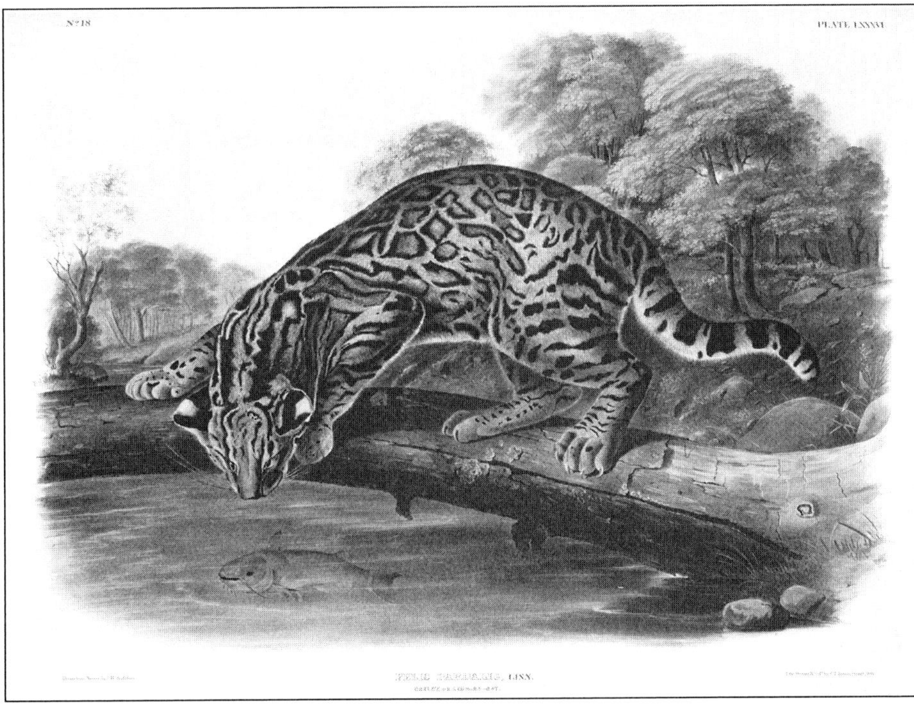

Fig. 6. John James Audubon, *Ocelot or Leopard-cat, Felis Paradis, Linn. (Male)*. (1845/1848), in: *The Viviparous Quadrupeds of North America*, Vol II, Plate LXXXVI. © The Trustees of the Natural History Museum, London.

the most expensive book in the world. Audubon was notable for his expansive studies and his detailed illustrations of animals in their natural habitats. His graphics can function as a source of friction for Taryn Simon's picture of the *White Tiger (Kenny)*.[29] The panthera (fig. 5) crouches slightly, head down, and one paw extended before his body, as if pausing in the midst of his movement. This is an ideal capture for an observer to study this extremely rare creature – its physique, its muscles, its coat. This posture is oddly similar to the one John James Audubon chose for his depiction of an Ocelot (fig. 6), which he presented in his second volume of *The Viviparous Quadrupeds of North America* (1845-1848). But Kenny's cage, lacking all

29 Simon 2008 (as note 2), 75.

traces of nature, counteracts the idealized environment of the hunting wildcat. Adding the information from the text, we learn that the living animal is itself an 'artificial product', just as the drawn one (or the fantastic and exotic creatures of the *Physiologus*) in search for an 'ideal' – and that it is judged by the same quality standards:

> In the U.S. all living white tigers are the result of selective inbreeding in captivity to artificially create the genetic conditions that lead to white fur, ice-blue eyes and a pink nose. [...] As a result of inbreeding, Kenny has mental retardation and significant physical limitations. Due to his deep-set nose, he has difficulty breathing and closing his jaw [...]. Currently inbreeding such as father to daughter, brother to sister, mother to son has become common place. It produces a white cub less than 25% of the time, with only approximately 3% of those considered 'quality'. The three other tigers of Kenny's litter are not considered to be quality white tigers as they are yellow coated, cross eyed, and knock-kneed.[30]

The subject of Kenny points out the shift from admiring species-appropriate behavior of wildlife to its exploitation by a celebrated entertainment culture, which has to be served at all costs. At the same time, it shows, that – beside an apparently neutral list of facts, which provide information – the paragraphs of the *American Index* deal with and communicate moral standards. Though Taryn Simon states that she tries to "keep [her] opinion or any sort of political slam outside of the work",[31] it is the choice of which information is given and which key words are used that these *epigrams* can be regarded as carefully composed rhetorical devices, just as the *subscriptio* in emblem books. The text evokes compassion and empathy for Kenny's destiny by counting his retardations. It further evokes disgust by lengthily listing the possible incestuous arrangements. By stressing his status as a living creature

30 Simon 2008 (as note 2), 75.

31 Nicole Davis, "Taryn Simon", on: *Artnet TV* [05. April 2010], http://www.youtube.com/watch?v=xBuY1lsUXkc#t=31 (accessed 26 August 2014).

32 Steinaecker 2007 (as note 19), 87 [translated by author].

33 Coggins 2008 (as note 4).

34 Simon 2008 (as note 2), 133.

with a given name and an individual fate, the considerations of him as a commodity of a certain value cause resistance.
This is repeated in the picture, in which a subtle reference to an (art historical) icon adds a moral connotation as well. In this manner, *pictura* and *epigram* in Simon's work therefore share the "moralistic-didactic tendencies, which are traditionally inherent in the emblematic as 'didactic poetry'".[32]

*

Although Taryn Simon was allowed to take pictures inside the CIA Headquarters (p. 42/43), a Screening Room of the Church of Scientology (p. 129) and the Imperial Office of the World Knights of the Ku Klux Klan (p. 73), organizations associated with high standards of secrecy, a few companies turned down her request.[33] One prominent yet rather unexpected example marks the closure of *An American Index of the Hidden and Unfamiliar*: Disneyland denied Taryn Simon access behind the scenes, where, for example, the staff dress as the beloved characters and the tons of waste the resort produces on a daily basis are taken care of. So instead of a *pictura-epigram* combination, the last page only shows the excerpt from Disney's response in the lower right corner (fig. 7), resembling a period at the end of a statement (or the signature on a work of art) on a otherwise blank spread:

> After giving your request serious consideration, even though it is against company policy to consider such a request, it is with regret that I inform you that we are not willing to grant the permission you seek.... As you are aware, our Disney characters, parks and other valuable properties have become beloved by young and old alike, and with this comes a tremendous responsibility to protect their use and the protection we currently enjoy. Should we lapse in our vigilance, we run the risk of losing this protection and the Disney characters as we know and love them. Especially during these violent times, I personally believe that the magical spell cast on guests who visit our theme parks is particularly important to protect and helps to provide them with an important fantasy they can escape to.[34]

The modified structure and content of the page radicalizes the concept of the "Leerstelle":[35] The blank space, as a significant quasi invisible *pictura*,

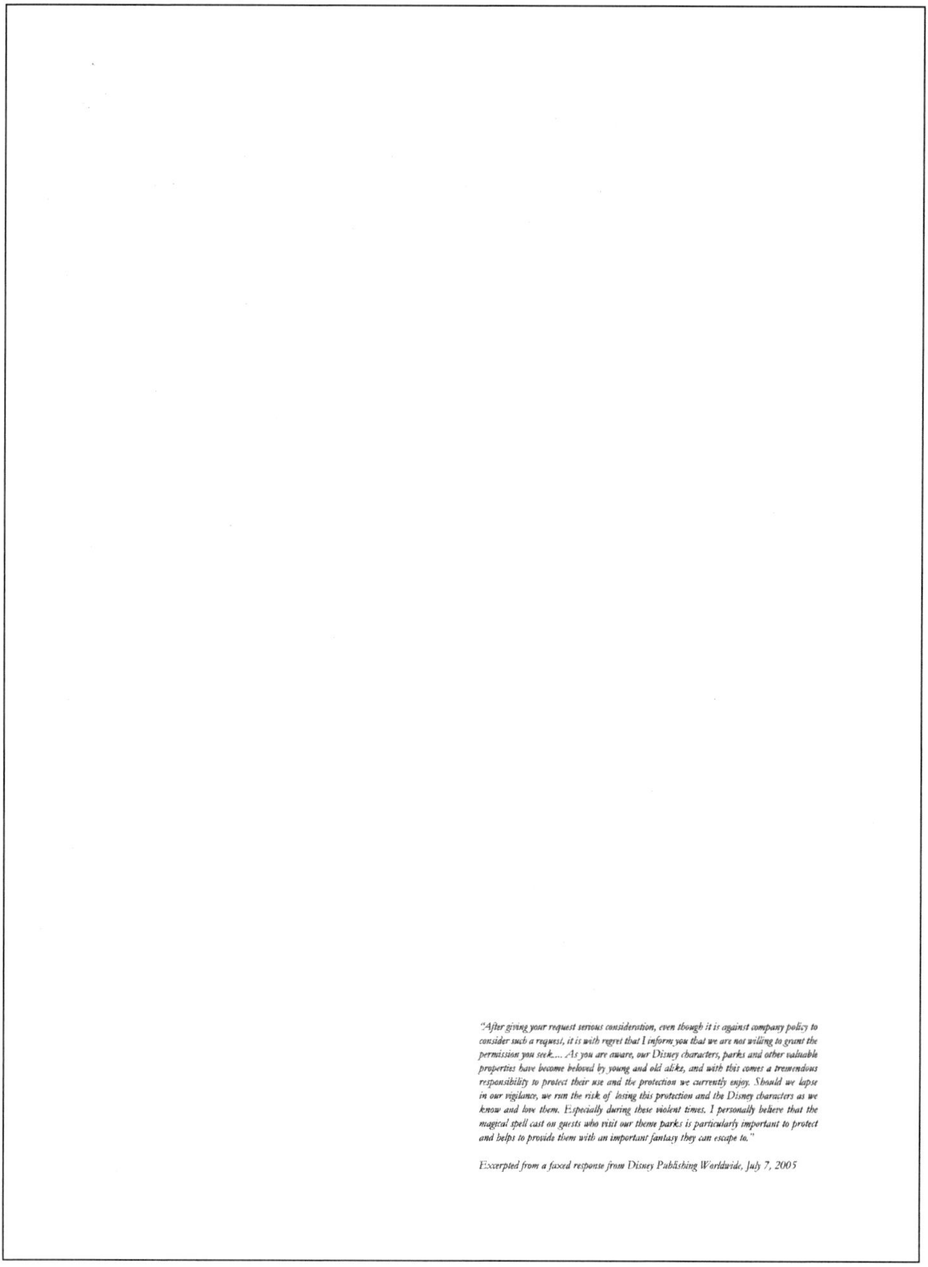

"After giving your request serious consideration, even though it is against company policy to consider such a request, it is with regret that I inform you that we are not willing to grant the permission you seek.... As you are aware, our Disney characters, parks and other valuable properties have become beloved by young and old alike, and with this comes a tremendous responsibility to protect their use and the protection we currently enjoy. Should we lapse in our vigilance, we run the risk of losing this protection and the Disney characters as we know and love them. Especially during these violent times. I personally believe that the magical spell cast on guests who visit our theme parks is particularly important to protect and helps to provide them with an important fantasy they can escape to."

Excerpted from a faxed response from Disney Publishing Worldwide, July 7, 2005

Fig. 7. Taryn Simon, *Excerpted from a faxed response from Disney publishing Worldwide, July 7, 2005*, 2007. Reprod. from Taryn Simon, *An American Index of the Hidden and Unfamiliar*, 2nd ed., Göttingen 2008, p. 133. © Taryn Simon. Courtesy Gagosian Gallery.

offers room for reflection and invites to 'fill in' one's own 'pictures' and associations. The reader/viewer "is faced with a whole network of possibilities, and thus himself begins to formulate missing links. The temporary withholding of information acts as a stimulus, and this is further intensified by details suggestive of possible solutions. The blanks make the reader himself bring the story to life."[36]

This *story* – or in this case: the imaginary picture – will be influenced by the given text, not least because of the personal appeal (*your request, I inform you, the permission you seek, As you are aware*). In this means, the content of the text contains the *details suggestive of possible solutions* and becomes the "trace"[37] of what is invisible.[38]

*

The choice for the closing page also revisits and subtly increases the utilization of the "symbol of obvious national significance and graphic strength"[39] used for the opening page. For the entertainment park is not merely an American icon, but rather, according to Baudrillard,

35 The concept of the 'Leerstelle' was "introduced, with some hesitancy, into the terminology of art history from that of literary criticism. In the works of Roman Ingarden and Wolfgang Iser, respectively, this concept is referred to as 'place of indeterminacy' and 'blank' or 'gap'." Wolfgang Kemp and Raymond Meyer, "Death at Work: A Case Study on Constitutive Blanks in Nineteenth-Century Painting", in: *Representations* 10 (Spring, 1985), 102-123, here 107.

36 Wolfgang Iser, *The Act of Reading: A Theory of Aesthetic Response*, Baltimore/London 1978, 297, quoted after: Kemp/Meyer 1985 (as note 35), 116.

37 Kemp/Meyer 1985 (as note 35), 112.

38 The iconic virtue of such offered space is distinct in the observations of Peter de Voogd on the blank page in Laurence Sterne's *The Life and Opinions of Tristram Shandy, Gentleman* (1759-1767). Though Sterne explicitly encourages his readers to draw their own image of a certain character from the chapter on the intentionally left blank page, de Voogd states that he has not found one single drawing in over six hundred observed copies of *Tristram Shandy*. The imaginary figure, changeable, fluent, and complex, apparently stays more potent when not constricted and fixed through outlines. De Voogd even addresses this blank page in Sterne's book as an emblem itself: a "colorless counterpart" to the marbled leaves, which Sterne himself describes "as the 'motley emblem' of his work". Peter de Voogd, "Laurence Sterne's Blank Emblem", in: *Living in Posterity. Essays in Honour of Bart Westerweel*, ed. Jan Frans van Dijkhuizen, Hilversum 2004, 315-332, here 317 (I thank Prof. Sabine Mödersheim for pointing out this article to me).

39 Exh. cat. Washington 2009 (as note 9), 177.

> [t]he objective profile of the United States [...] may be traced throughout Disneyland, even down to the morphology of individuals and the crowd. All its values are exalted here, in miniature and comic-strip form. Embalmed and pacified. [A] digest of the American way of life, panegyric to American values, idealized transportation of a contradictory reality.[40]

In this perspective, the brief *epigram* is more than the final chord to the *American Index*. It enables us to transfer the discussed topics onto a wider prospective, in terms of what has been observed as well on what is still unseen. This is also initiated by the divergence in terms of form and content. It is the only page where only the operator of a represented site has their say. In this, the main themes of the foregone pages are directly or indirectly addressed in a concentrated form: restriction of access and therefore restriction of knowledge for the private individual, both the revealing and suggestive power of the image, and the replacement of a maybe inconvenient reality with a comforting facade. The request to take pictures is treated like an act of violation and the corporate management answers this with key terms, associated with a threat to peace and well-being, as well as measures to react to such: *violent*

40 Jean Baudrillard, "Simulacra and Simulations", in: *Selected Writings*, ed. Mark Poster, 2nd ed., Stanford 2007, 171-172.

41 Jean Baudrillard, "Disneyworld Company", in: *Liberation* March 4 (1996), 5.

42 Jeff Ferrell, *Tearing down the Streets. Adventures in Urban Anarchy*, New York 2002, 8.

43 http://en.wikipedia.org/wiki/Disneyfication (accessed 26 August 2014). This quoted extract from a highly frequented online-encyclopedia is not only part of their definition of the cultural and socio-architectural phenomenon of 'Disneyfication', but also just the opposite to "Hidden and Unfamiliar". The term 'Disneyfication'/'Disneyization' is applied for a spreading culture which is, according to Alan Bryman, characterized through 'theming' (i.e. objects largely unrelated to the applied institution), 'hybrid consumption' (originally definite consumptions becoming difficult to distinguish), 'merchandising' and 'performative labour' (frontline service work being viewed as performance). It is also described by Jeff Ferrel as "a powerful metaphor for the insidious sanitization of urban life, and as a political economic reality underwriting the closure of urban space." Ferrell 2002 (as note 42), 8. – Alan Bryman, *The Disneyization of Society*, London 2004, 2.

44 David Graham, "Turning the Accomplishment of many Years into an Hour-Glass: Lessons from the History of Emblem Studies", Plenary Lecture at the 10th International Conference of the *Society for Emblem Studies* held at Kiel University, July 2014.

45 See Peter M. Daly, *Emblem Theory. Recent German Contributions to the Characterization of the Emblem Genre*, Nendeln 1979, 74.

times, risk of losing (something/someone we *love*), *vigilance, tremendous responsibility, escape,* and multiple forms of *to protect.*

This reaction is an involuntary cynical commentary on the intention of the *American Index,* namely, to explore the existing blind spots within American society and to question their accessibility for the public. It highlights even more an intentional act of hiding: to cast a *magical spell* on somebody is used as euphemism for keeping somebody in ignorance, whereas photography is seemingly assigned the role of a medium for the communication of (unwanted) knowledge. The authority over what is visible and which external perception is generated through this (as well as which moral standards and social values are projected), is in the possession of a minority. This results in an incapacitation of a majority relieved of the decisions which come with knowledge. For this purpose, no other image than the facade is permitted to exist. And although there is undoubtedly a life behind the scenes and that there are human beings inside those cartoonish costumes, the company managed to remove this fact from the public mind on the grounds of the *company policy* quoted above. "[Disney] is [...] interested in erasing the real by turning it into a three-dimensional virtual image with no depth".[41] Their existence is reduced to a "sanitized"[42] facade, and so the deployed *fantasy* is the reality. Considering the fact that this strategy played a major part in Disney's global success, the last page additionally challenges the costumer's share of responsibility of those fantasies, which is again expressed by the layout and the text, as shown above. Is the triumphant advance of such enterprises as Disney the result of acceptance, ignorance or resignation to opacity? Do we want to know, or do we want to stick to "subject[s] more pleasant and easily grasped"?[43]

*

This last question is implied on every page of the *American Index,* which utilizes the emblematic strategy to follow the emblematic intention "to draw the reader into a self-reflective examination of his or her own life."[44] The locations, the inventory, the people, and likewise the facts and figures are – as the word and the image of an emblem[45] – presented as symbols, allegories, and indices themselves. The *picturae* are not only the concrete images of what can be seen; they also refer to something outside the frame. Thus, they own ontological (through the medium of photography) as well as semantic qualities (through their references). They manifest something abstract and visually suggest ways to think of unimaginable things, such as the idea of a religious belief (for example p. 29, 41, 45). The *epigrams* with concrete numbers and broad references beyond the images signify the possible and/or existing consequences for the contemporary society as an "unforgiving anchor"[46] to reality.

Lastly, the individual constituent elements of the title (*Index, Hidden, Unfamiliar*) and their meanings, as explained in the beginning, are omnipresent on each page and can consequently be seen as a superordinated *motto/lemma* for each of the subjects.[47] Under this *lemma*, the intentionally unsorted and miscellaneous topics as well as the alternating main themes clasp – similar to a traditional emblem book. For although their emblems are arranged in a particular order, they can be understood of their own accord and not necessarily depend on the previous or following ones, but are always tied to the overall intention expressed in the title or chapter. The intention of *The American Index of the Hidden and Unfamiliar* is to look behind the eagerly presented comforting facades and it withholds the offered easy *escape*, that lies in accepting or ignoring them. In this way, the "anxiety we feel when these strange worlds are unhidden"[48] may more likely be the result of the generated emblematic synergy evoking the mechanisms of the uncanny: *nothing new or alien*, but the gladly repressed understanding that those *strange worlds* and phenomena are logical consequences and concomitants of already visible and known circumstances is disturbing.

46 Coggins 2008 (as note 4).

47 With regard to the emblematic title-page Höltgen observed, that "[i]n some cases the words of the title itself may be regarded as the Lemma"; Karl Josef Höltgen, "Early Modern English Emblematic Title-Pages and their Cultural Context", in: *Entrée aus Schrift und Bild. Titelblatt und Frontispiz im England der Neuzeit*, eds. Werner Busch, Hubertus Fischer and Joachim Möller, Münster 2008, 41.

48 Ronald Dworkin, "Commentary", in: Simon 2008 (as note 2), 145.

The Concept of Inner-Pictorial Serial Structures in the Works of the ZERO Group

LAURA WEBER

Light, motion and space – these phenomenological aspects that leveraged the ZERO artists to increase the objectivity and non-figurative reflect a modern and dynamic world-view. The aspect of serial structures is indeed inherent while dealing with these phenomena in the artworks of ZERO, but it has only been discussed to a very small extent so far.[1] In its entirety, this aspect still constitutes a desideratum for research.

According to the structuralist Lévi-Strauss, "the property of a system of signs is to be transformable, in other words translatable, into the language of another system with the help of substitutions."[2] Hence, the system of language itself is translatable into a system of visual signs and structure. Language and structures in artworks can be analyzed structurally as well as syntactically. The objective of this paper is to analyze the serial structures of selected artworks by the ZERO group by considering them as analogous to language structures.

1 For the state of research see Laura Weber, *Zur seriellen Struktur in der Malerei und Objektkunst der 1950/60er Jahre*, PhD dissertation University of Kiel, forthcoming.

2 Claude Lévi-Strauss, *Structural Anthropology*, vol. 2, trans. Monique Layton, Chicago 1983, 19. – See Kornelia von Berswordt-Wallrabe, *Gerhard von Gravenitz – Eine Kunst jenseits des Bildes*, Ostfildern 1994, 49.

Structure and Language

The term 'structure', derived from the Latin word *structura*, means to arrange different parts of something into a pattern or system in which each part is connected to the others. As abstract as this definition may seem, structures are encountered in each scientific discipline, applying their own and proper methodology in order to decipher and conceive the system of the topic to be investigated. According to artist and art theorist Kepes, "[from] inorganic structures to plants and animals, from the movements of animals to their social behavior patterns and to human relations, structure is central."[3]
With regard to visual arts, structure is an inherent principle to arrange the pictorial content. Since the beginning of the 20th century, stylistic means such as perspective, proportions or hierarchical arrangements have progressively lost their importance within pictorial language. Composition in its traditional sense was replaced by abstract expressions or concrete ideas, which put emphasis on visual perception rather than representational qualities. Following geometric or tectonic laws, henceforth, the artistic means of expression became *structure*.
According to Max Bill, the essential characteristic of concrete art in particular is structure, which is ruled by "the series, the rhythm, the progression, the polarity, the regularity, the inner logic of sequence and arrangement".[4] Within the context of ZERO, elements condensed into series, such as points, lines and grids, form the structure and imagery of an artwork.
The introductory assumption by Lévi-Strauss opens up the opportunity for the convergence of different scientific methods.[5] The system of language allows to express thoughts and feelings. It is an important and typal means of communication. According to Saussure, language is a formal system of signs, a system of mandatory rules and conventions within a linguistic community.[6]

3 György Kepes, "Introduction", in: *Structure in art and in science*, ed. György Kepes, New York 1965, i-iii, here iii.
4 Max Bill [1959], quoted in Margit Staber, "Concrete Painting as Structural Painting", in: Kepes 1965 (as note 3), 165-185, here 172.
5 See Berswordt-Wallrabe 1994 (as note 2), 50.
6 See Ferdinand de Saussure, *Grundfragen der allgemeinen Sprachwissenschaft*, eds. Charles Bally and Albert Riedlinger, trans. Hermann Lommel, 3rd ed., Berlin 2001, 80.

Linguistics is the study of language in general and of particular languages, their structure, grammar and history. Structuralist linguistics focuses on the determination and description of single units of this system (such as sounds, word elements and words or phrases) and the relationships between them.[7] The key aspects of the transfer from language to visual structures are the rules for the internal structure of phrases and sentences, which is called syntax. Syntax, meaning *to arrange* or *order*, is the study of rules allowing to combine smaller linguistic units of different complexity such as words and phrases to form grammatical sentences.[8] In summary, syntax is a systematic arrangement. The semantic aspect of language, which constitutes the meaning of signs, is, however, excluded in the ongoing analysis. The order and arrangement of structural units already indicates that similarities to serial structures in art are given on a formal level. It is the purpose of the following analysis to compare the characteristics of both systems, (serial) structures and language.

Artistic Positions

Heinz Mack

The concept of serial arrangement is applied in Heinz Mack's work series called *Dynamische Strukturen* [Dynamic Structures]. The medium, mostly canvas or nettle, is given a serially striped structure by applying synthetic resin, usually in white color on a darker ground.[9] The liquid resin is treated with windshield wipers, squeegees or palette knives that create a more or less regular rhythm of white stripes allowing the dark background to be partially uncovered again.

The exemplary untitled *Dynamic Structure* from 1959 (fig. 1) shows that Mack also applied this concept to other artistic media such as lithogra-

7 See Bernd Kortmann, *Linguistik: Essentials. Anglistik, Amerikanistik*, Berlin 1999, 12.

8 See Kortmann 1999 (as note 7), 89.

9 See Thomas Beck, "Licht als Thema im Werk von Heinz Mack. Eine Analyse der ästhetischen Grundlagen", in: *Zero-Studien. Aufsätze zur Düsseldorfer Gruppe ZERO und ihrem Umkreis* (Karlsruher Studien zur Kunstgeschichte, vol. 2), ed. Klaus Gereon Beuckers, Münster 1997, 11-51, here 13.

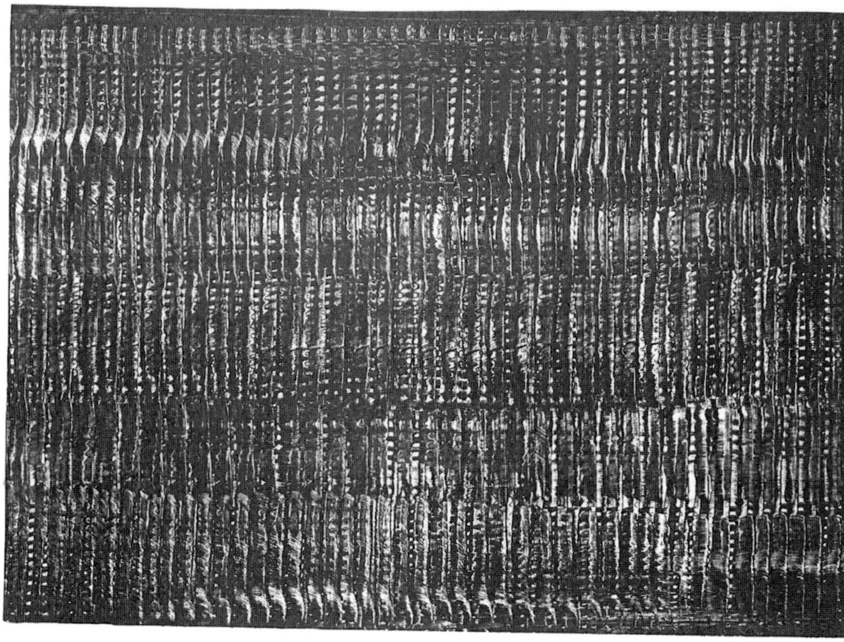

Fig. 1. Heinz Mack, *Untitled (Dynamische Struktur)*, 1959, lithograph, 50 x 65 cm. Collection Lenz Schönberg, Söll/Tirol. © VG Bild-Kunst, Bonn 2014. Photo: Archiv Lenz Schönberg.

phy.[10] Here, Mack chose a black ground on which white color was applied in a striped structure. It consists of vertical lines, arranged in an irregular and variable manner. Their shape depends on the amount of white paint and on how much pressure was exerted within the manual production process. The interplay of white paint and black ground generates light-dark contrasts, causing a virtual motion. The light stripes optically step forward, creating a visual movement that projects into space. Heinz Mack stated in his essay "The new dynamic structure" that movement would "not only be realized on the surface of the painting but [would] also leap out at the observer unexpectedly."[11]

The vibrating space between the beholder and the painting itself is caused by the structured light, which is experienced as a visual phenomenon. Light and dark contrasts as well as the width and depth variations initiate an optical dynamization of the artwork, causing flickering effects and an overstimulation of the observer, while changing the perspective in front of the painting. It seems as if the structured surface takes off and floats above the medium. This creates a concrete form in the virtual space, a three-dimensional volume that visually approaches the beholder.

The serial structure appears to be open towards the edges, and gives the impression as if the rhythmic structure might endlessly continue beyond the boundaries. This impression is only disrupted by the broad margin of the medium on which the structure was printed. The pictorial effect of the dynamic structure is obtained by the active beholder. He or she is therefore an essential part of the artwork and its underlying concept. Without its beholder, the visual perception could not be triggered, and therefore the artwork not be completed. This redefines the relation between work and its recipient.

The perceived structure in Heinz Mack's *Dynamic Structure* resembles in its varying rhythm, due to the differing execution of stripes and their subtly nuanced chromaticity, written language and its formal ordering of words, varying in length and composition. Following the horizontal reading direction from left to right (or the other way round), the sequence of vertical stripes as well as the sequence of words create a rhythmic flow of abstract information.

Günther Uecker

Instead of paint, Günther Uecker chose the conventional nail as his most famous structural element. He hammered his serial arrangements of nails directly onto the image surface. Mostly being painted over with white color,

10 Besides lithography, Mack also translated this method by applying its principles onto aluminium plates. On his light-reliefs or light-stelae the incident light is easily refracted by their structured surfaces and directly reflected towards the experiencing beholder.

11 Heinz Mack's essay "The new dynamic structure" was published in the first edition of the ZERO magazine in 1958 on the occasion of the seventh evening exhibition. Heinz Mack, "Die neue dynamische Struktur" [1958], in: *ZERO*, eds. Heinz Mack and Otto Piene, Köln 1973, 14-15, here 15. – See also Udo Kultermann, "Der neue Dynamismus in der Malerei. Bemerkungen zu Bildern von Mack und Piene", in: *ZERO 4321*, eds. Dirk Pörschmann and Mattijs Visser, Düsseldorf 2012, 405-409.

the nails visualize interactions of light and shade. The beholder, again an integral part of the artwork itself, experiences the visual movement of the structure.

Till the end of the 1950s, Uecker's early nail works are characterized by a rather strict and symmetrical arrangement, based on mathematical series. These structural rigidities have been loosened since the beginning of the 1960s.[12] From this time onward, he chose the position of the nails more randomly, as in *Weißes Feld* from 1966 (fig. 2). Working from the middle outwards, the irregular arrangement of nails set in various angles and density creates the impression of a spiral motion, intensified by the interplay of light and shadows cast. Due to the length of the nails, the material stands out from the surface and constitutes another pulsating virtual surface structure.

"Although I use nails as structural elements I do not want them seen as nails. By putting these means in an ordered relationship to each other I want to set them vibrating thereby disturbing and confusing their geometrical order."[13] The inclined arrangement of nails creates the illusion of a delicate and soft rhythmic movement and thereby contradicts not only the rigid material but also the strenuous effort of the noisy production process. The dynamic structure of *Weißes Feld* recalls tall reed swaying in the wind. Here, the title additionally evokes associations with nature.

Günther Uecker's nail art created a visual language that is focused on changeability and sensitising the beholder's perception. Similar to the syntactical order of written language, the nail arrangements follow a systematic pattern. The rigid structure of the all-over pattern is loosened by the wavy surface of ordered nails that create a visual, sinuous rhythm. The perception of the undulating and gradual movement brings the nail structures even closer to spoken language patterns, resembling acoustic waves and speech melodies.

12 Günther Uecker, "Der Zustand Weiß" [1961], in: *Zero aus Deutschland 1957-1966 und heute*, exh.cat. Galerie der Stadt Esslingen/Villa Merkel Esslingen, ed. Renate Wiehager, Ostfildern 2000, 251.

13 Uecker [1961] 2000 (as note 12), 145.

14 See Ursula Perucchi-Petri, "Otto Piene and Zero", in: *Otto Piene*, ed. Ante Glibota, Paris 2011, 253-267, here 263. – See Beate Fricke, "Rauch und Feuer bei Otto Piene", in: Beuckers 1997 (as note 9), 53-82, here 55.

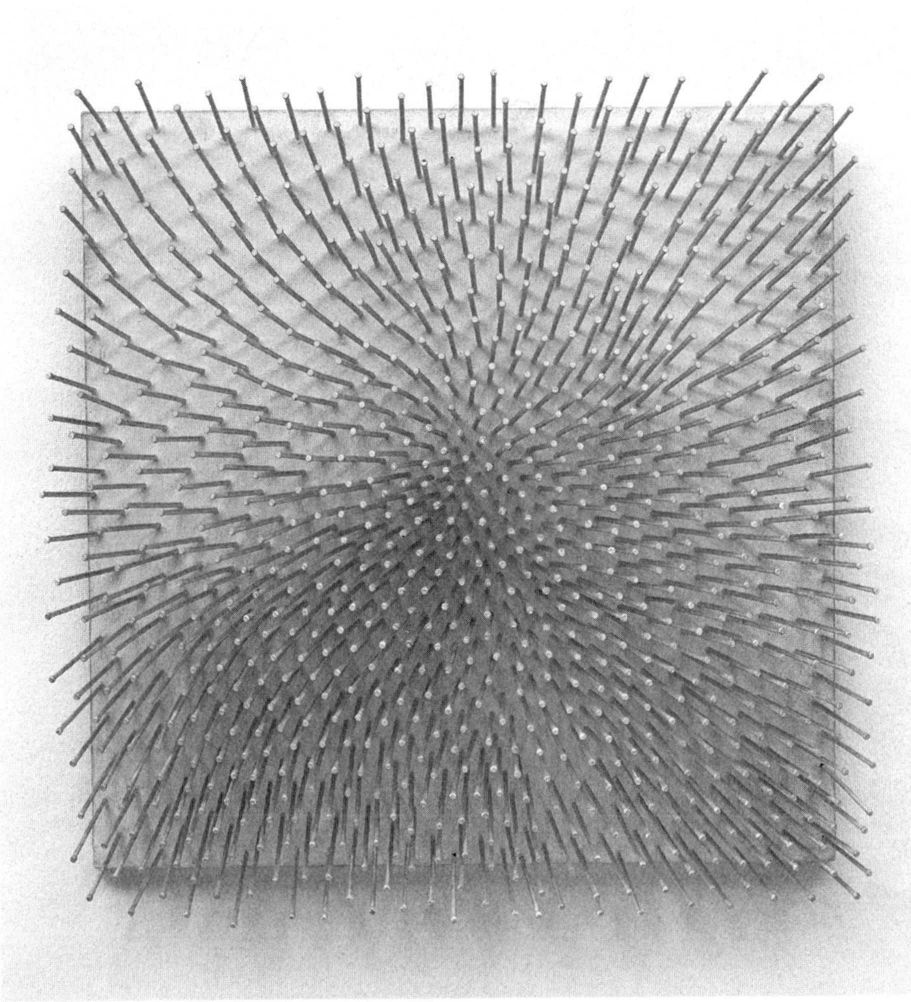

Fig. 2. Günther Uecker, *Weißes Feld*, 1966, 50 x 50 cm. Formerly Collection Lenz Schönberg, Söll/Tirol, present owner unknown. © VG Bild-Kunst, Bonn 2014. Photo: Philipp Schönborn, München.

Otto Piene

By applying paint through customized raster grids made of carton or metal provided with holes directly onto the canvas, Piene achieved a preset serial structure of colored points standing out in relief from the homochromatic ground.[14]

Fig. 3. Otto Piene, *gelbgelbweißheißschnell*, 1958, oil on canvas, 127 x 162 cm. Collection Lenz Schönberg, Söll/Tirol. © VG Bild-Kunst, Bonn 2014. Photo: Philipp Schönborn, München.

Since 1957, Piene has worked on his first stencil paintings, exploring the visual effects of raster screenings as a new means of artistic production.[15] He chose the point or circle as his structural element, which is a recurrent thread throughout his entire oeuvre.[16] Early examples of stencil paintings are structured by a severe raster, i.e. they show a regularity with respect to the arrangement of points in quantity per row as well as the structural form.

Despite the rigid pattern of the point structure, the artwork itself seems dynamized, set in vibration and motion, because, upon closer inspection, it turns out that the raster shows slight irregularities. Furthermore, the incident light, refracted by the relief-like color points, is enabled to articulate itself on the well-reflecting surface. The effect is a vibrating surface on which the observing eye is vainly trying to focus and therefore set in constant motion.

As Fricke points out, Piene makes use of the figure-ground perception, a perceptual process whereby the two-dimensional image on the observer's retina is complemented by three-dimensional information.[17]

During the period of his raster paintings, Piene manufactured numerous different versions of stencils. They developed from more rigid geometric patterns into circular arrangements of holes, varying in density and regularity.[18] The stencil painting *gelbgelbweißheißschnell* from 1958 (fig. 3) illustrates a more complex arrangement of the applied point structure. Around the oval white centre of the yellow painting same-colored spots are loosely arranged in a semi-circular shape. The same structured accumulations of points are also applied right and left to the centre. Here, the sharp edges of the stencil are prominently visible and frame the flamboyant middle part of the painting.

Upon closer inspection, these edges seem to indicate the only usage of this particular stencil in order to structure the whole surface. While the centre is constructed by using the same stencil twice but rotated by 180 degrees, the surrounded area is shaped by the lower parts, displaying only segments of the stencil. The concept of seriality is here not only applied by the serially arranged point structure, but moreover by the repetitive usage of the same stencil. The stencil painting *gelbgelbweißheißschnell* therefore appears excerpt-like, taken from an infinitely extensible structure. Due to the title, the exemplary stencil painting *gelbgelbweißheißschnell* evokes associations with the sun or sunlight, which is additionally enforced by the applied semi-circular structure and color.

Parallel to his raster paintings, Piene worked on his smoke drawings, smoke paintings and his light ballets. While the visual effects in his smoke drawings

15 The use of semi-mechanical techniques such as Piene's raster screenings or Uecker's use of nails, enabled the ZERO artists to objectify the artistic process, trying to eliminate the influence of their artist's personality on their works. This new way of production served them in order to separate their artistic practice from the contemporaneous Informel painting, which was characterized by a more direct and therefore subjective expressiveness.

16 Piene's more recent ceramic works show a close relationship to his early stencil paintings. Here, Piene returns to the usage of grids and enhances this proven method by including color. See Ante Glibota, "Tactile Juxtaposition", in: Glibota 2011 (as note 14), 646 – 674, here 646.

17 See Fricke 1997 (as note 14), 55.

18 See Perucchi-Petri 2011 (as note 14), 265.

and paintings are created by billowing smoke of a candle or a kerosene lamp channelled through stencils leaving sequences of soot marks on the surface, Piene progressively overcame the pictorial space by projecting direct light sources into the real space. This systematic exploration of real space culminates in the environmental happenings of his Sky Art events.[19]

Whether in his raster paintings, smoke drawings and paintings or light ballets, Piene chose the rigid concept of predetermined stencils as his means of production to achieve a more or less regular pattern on his medium of choice. These almost monotone arrangements that Piene modifies to the very limits of the possible, create a visual dynamic that resembles text passages in its formal structure. Especially the rigid arrangements of his early works resemble in their formal structure a written text composed of sequences of single words stringed together in line structure and following a linear reading direction. Although the shape of circular patterns as in *gelbgelbweißheißschnell* does not follow a strict linear arrangement, and therefore visually differs from the formal structure of texts, the application of the structural elements is still based on the same underlying concept of serial arrangement.

Dadamaino

Similar to Otto Piene and the previous considerations, Dadamaino chose the point, circle or, to be precise, round cut-outs as her structural elements that were arranged in a severe grid pattern. Hence, the transferability of the applied structure to written texts is evident.

The implementation of serial structures in Dadamaino's works has undergone a change. Her early work is strongly influenced by Lucio Fontana's spatial concept and his slit or perforated monochrome paintings.[20] The works within the series *Volumi* consist of up to four large irregular and oval shaped

19 See Chris Gerbing, "'Mit 12 x 12 Scheinwerfern zum Mond' Die Universalität des Raumes in den Lichtbaletten und Sky Events von Otto Piene", in: Beuckers 1997 (as note 9), 83-111. – *Otto Piene. Sky Art 1968–1996*, eds. Susanne Rennert and Stephan von Wiese, Cologne 1999.

20 Francesco Tedeschi, "Dadamainos Werk. Von den frühen fünfziger Jahren bis zu den 'Fatti della Vita'", in: *Dadamaino. Retrospektive 1958 – 2000*, exh. cat. Museum Bochum, Bochum, eds. Hans Günter Golinski and Sepp Hiekisch-Picard, Bochum 2000, 13-43, here 18.

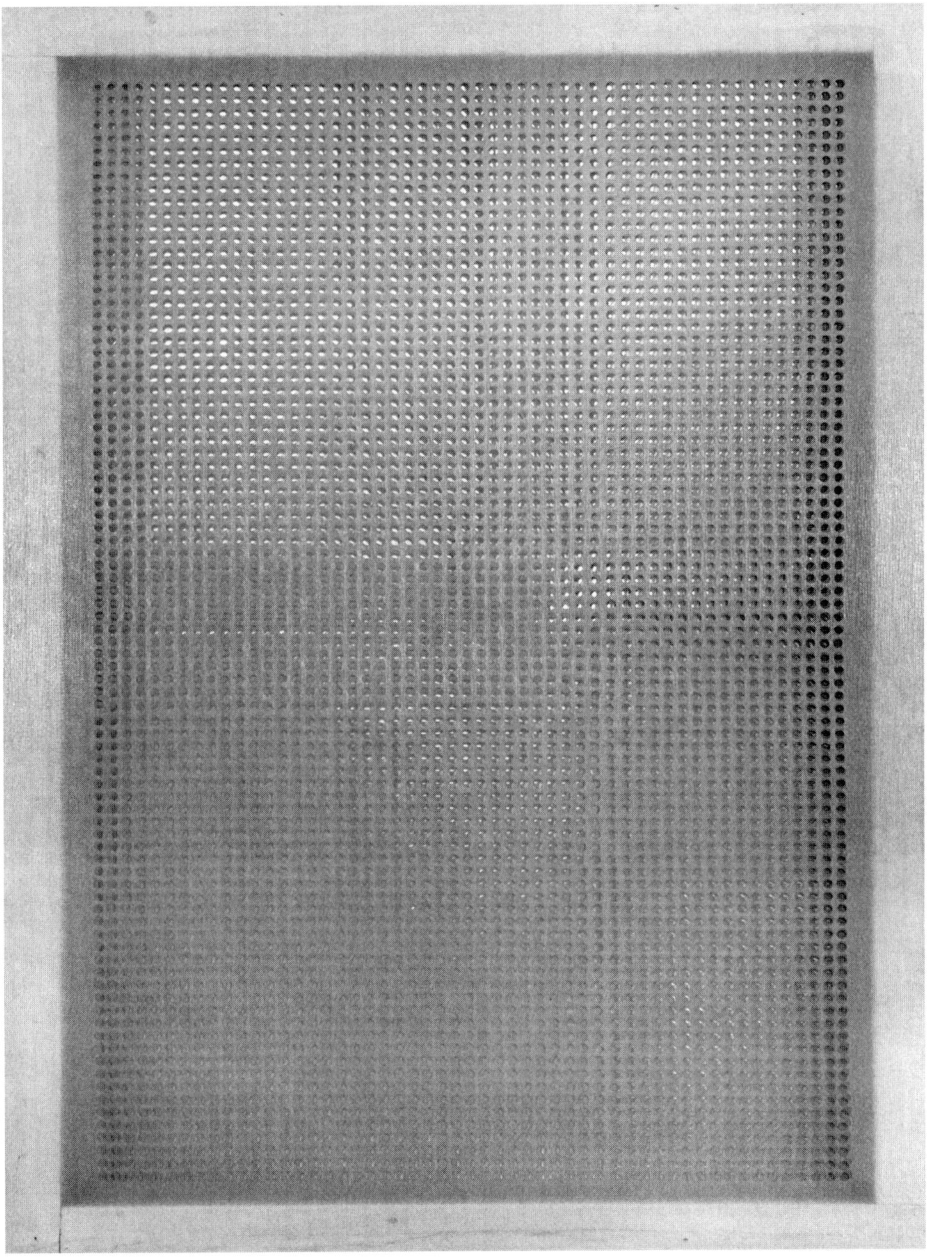

Fig. 4. Dadamaino, *Volume a moduli sfasati*, 1960, 150 x 100 cm, two-layered plastic foils punched by hand on double stretcher bars. Private collection, courtesy Archivio Dadamaino. © Archivio Dadamaino 2014. Photo: Luigi Acerra.

holes that almost occupy the entire monochrome painted surface. The result is, as the title suggests, a spatial volume evoked by the removal of material in order to withdraw any kind of reference but to reclaim purity.[21] Their shape evolves into circular holes that are arranged in horizontal as well as vertical sequences, followed by ascending or descending series.

Dadamaino's subsequent series can be seen as a further development of the *Volumi*. The technical title *Volumi a moduli sfasati* already refers to the applied technique: arranged in a regular grid pattern, Dadamaino perforated multiple plastic foils by a serial repetition of the structural element. Up to three or four of these perforated foils are layered and then applied onto the frame. However, slight irregularities are caused during these two processes. These irregularities provoke an overlapping of the applied point structure. The effect is a visually dynamic surface similar to Otto Piene's stencil paintings or smoke drawings. In addition, the virtual space enclosed by the applied grid pattern, and due to the perforated surface, is disclosed to the beholder.

The *Volumi a moduli sfasati* from 1960 (fig. 4) exemplifies Dadamaino's pursuit of overcoming the spatial restrictions of traditional media and her enduring interest in exploring new materials like plastic foils. Here, the serial arrangement of the structural element creates an impression of continuity. The applied structure based on its sequential arrangement is intellectually extensible *ad infinitum* and only defined by its framing on double stretcher bars. The use of serial structures as compositional elements is characteristic for the artistic perception of ZERO and Dadamaino in particular.

Gerhard von Graevenitz

Gerhard von Graevenitz not only borrows mathematical terms, such as *sequence*, *progression* or *distribution* as titles for his artworks but also uses their underlying methodologies. The new pictorial arrangement that he pursued in his works is no longer composed in a traditional sense, but "the problem

21 See Jole de Sanna, "Interview mit Dadamaino" (1995), in: *Zero Italien. Azimut/Azimuth 1959/60 in Mailand. Und heute*, exh.cat. Galerie der Stadt Esslingen/Villa Merkel, Esslingen, ed. Renate Damsch-Wiehager, Ostfildern 2000, 96-99, here 96.

22 Jürgen Morschel, "About Gerhard von Graevenitz" (1962), in: Exh. cat. Esslingen 2000 (as note 12), 176.

of contemporary painting is formulated as that of organizing quantities of anonymous elements instead of individual forms, replacing hierarchical order with statistical ones."[22]

Early versions of von Graevenitz's work series *Weiße Strukturen* [White Structures] are characterized by hierarchical orders. He organizes regular series of progressions, i.e. modulations of one single structural element (circular or rectangular) in size and order, both in the horizontal and vertical axis of the artwork, by embossing the structure into the material.[23] Due to displaced arrangements, single or multiple centres are formed on one surface.[24]

The incident light is refracted by the manually applied structure and articulates itself – similar to Uecker's nail art, Mack's light-reliefs or Piene's stencil paintings – in light and shade effects upon the monochrome white. This creates, again, both the experience of a visual and vibrating space.

The inclusion of the concept of random distribution enables von Graevenitz to obtain a more rigid, non-hierarchical homogeneous structure or, according to Frank Popper, to gain control of the microstructure.[25] This visual harmonizing of the microstructure automatically excludes any form of progression within an individual artwork. *Weiße Struktur, Regelmäßige Verteilung 1* from 1960/61 (fig. 5) is defined by the arrangement of alternating hemispherical cavities and concavities. Whereas progressions complicate the process of structuring a surface, here, it is sufficient for von Graevenitz to alternate rigid sequences of one and the same structural element in its positive and negative form. The existence of two companion pieces to *Weiße Struktur, Regelmäßige Verteilung 1* exemplifies that von Graevenitz extended the concept of progressing structures within an individual artwork to a work series.[26] Hence, each version is arranged in the same sequence of the structural element, but reduced in size in consecutive ascending order. According to the title, the work's central theme in von Graevenitz's *White Structures* is structure itself. The process of artistic creativity is almost com-

23 See Berswordt-Wallrabe 1994 (as note 2), 41.
24 See Morschel [1962] 2000 (as note 22), 176.
25 See Frank Popper, *Die Kinetische Kunst. Licht und Bewegung, Umweltkunst und Aktion*, Köln 1975, 32.
26 See Berswordt-Wallrabe 1994 (as note 2), 45.

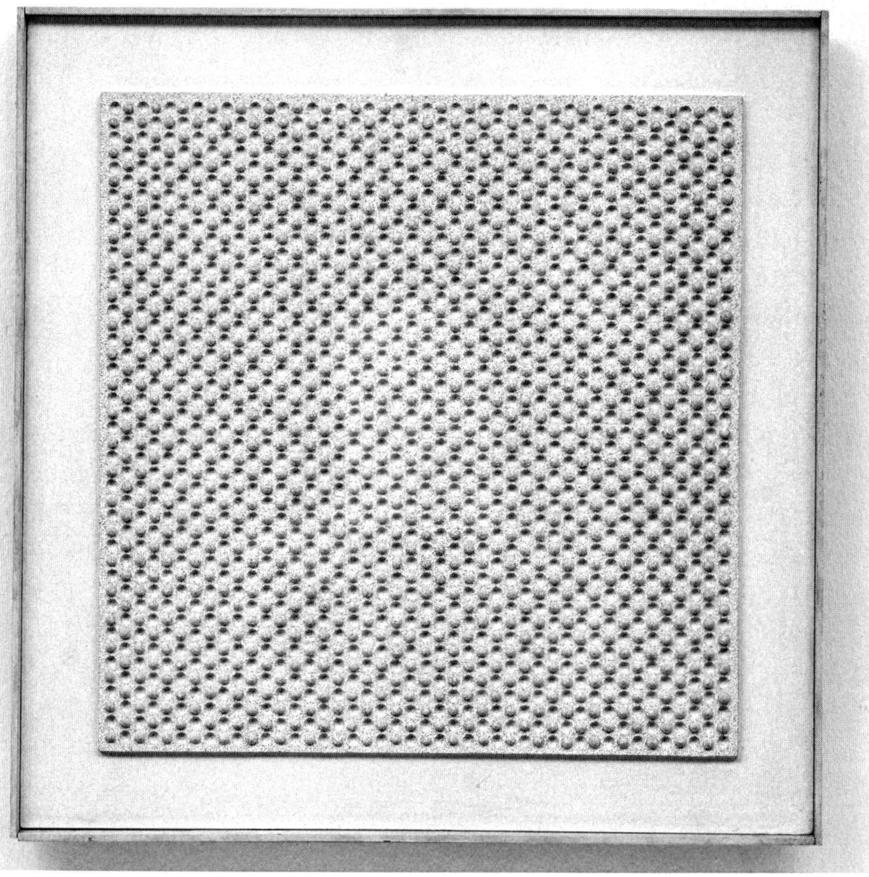

Fig. 5. Gerhard von Graevenitz, *Weiße Struktur, Regelmäßige Verteilung 1*, 1960/61, 50 x 50 cm, glue, wood flour, barite and crayon on wood. Formerly Collection Lenz Schönberg, Söll/Tirol, present owner unknown. © VG Bild-Kunst, Bonn 2014. Photo: Philipp Schönborn, München.

pletely suppressed: while the conditions are predetermined by the artist himself (namely form and size of the structural element, potential application of a positive or negative progression and the arrangement), the pattern has to follow the conceptual and systematic order.[27] The systematic arrangement of the same or alternating elements, here used in order to make aspects like space, material, color and light perceptible for the beholder, resemble a binary code that has to be translated.

Jan Schoonhoven

Since the formation of the Dutch group *Nul,* Schoonhoven has ended his painterly oeuvre and focused ever since on drawings as well as on serial and formally reduced reliefs. The exclusive concentration on the use of the monochrome white offered a well-reflecting surface on which incident light could articulate itself optimally.[28] The interaction of incident light and the applied structure in Schoonhoven's reliefs creates light and shade effects, which become an integral compositional element.

The internal structure in *Weißes Strukturrelief R 62-1* from 1962 (fig. 6) is based on a strict and binding grid structure. According to an additive principle, the relief is constructed by sequences of horizontal and vertical bars forming uniform rectangular-shaped cells. The apparently infinite repetition of the internal structure in Schoonhoven's white papier maché relief is limited by its broad framing and superordinate macro structure.[29] The material of his choice was papier maché or cardboard, a less expensive material that he coated with white emulsion paint. Upon closer inspection, it turns out that Schoonhoven's raster also shows slight irregularities, due to the manual handling of the sculptural material. Unlike Piene or von Graevenitz, Schoonhoven never wanted to ban the subjective factor from the individual handwriting.[30] His work therefore seems less industrially manufactured than, for example, Piene's stencil paintings, which resemble dotted linoleum flooring and certainly could have been perfected to that extent.

The ambivalence of serial arrangements and irregularities due to manual production evokes the tension of Schoonhoven's white reliefs.[31] Although

27 See Berswordt-Wallrabe 1994 (as note 2), 57-62.

28 See Renate Wiehager, "Nul 1960 – 1965. Und Heute", in: *Die niederländische Gruppe Nul 1960-1965 und heute,* exh. cat, Galerie der Stadt Esslingen/Villa Merkel, Esslingen, ed. Renate Damsch-Wiehager, Ostfildern 1993, 9. – Monochromy is characteristic for ZERO, since the limitation to a single color not only points out the overcoming of polychromy but also color contrasts that marked Informel painting. See Perucchi-Petri 2011 (as note 14), 266.

29 Bernhard Kerber: "Nul", in: Exh. cat. Esslingen 1993 (as note 28), 13.

30 Jan Schoonhoven, "Beflügeltes Weiß", in: Exh. cat. Esslingen 1993 (as note 28), 116-121, here 119.

31 See Juliane Bardt, *Kunst aus Papier. Zur Ikonographie eines plastischen Werkmaterials der zeitgenössischen Kunst,* Hildesheim 2006, 56.

the relief is based on a geometric grid pattern, the all-over structure does not appear to be monotone but vibrant. The systematic accumulation of geometric elements organized in a grid pattern resembles in terms of its structure linguistic regularity.
The analysis pictured only a rather small selection of artists and their usage of serial structures. Within the international network of ZERO, further artists like Piero Manzoni, Enrico Castellani, Jan Henderikse or followers of the Nouveau Réalisme like Arman, to name only a few, applied the concept of serial structures in their oeuvres. This demonstrates the vital exchange of artistic and aesthetic ideas during that period of time.

Visual Structures as Emblematic Strategies

Coming back to the question raised, namely to point out the similarities as well as the differences between both systems of language and serial structures in art, it can be concluded that sequences of structural elements in their entirety form a whole, a structure that is in its syntactical arrangement comparable to language. A language consists of serial arrangements of signs that form words that form sentences, and sentences that form textual bodies.
Furthermore, due to the serial arrangement of same or similar structural elements, a rhythmic sequence is evoked, comparable to a textual design. The more uniformly the structural elements are formed, the more weakened or monotone the rhythm becomes, resulting in an arrangement of one and the same unit, such as a uniform point structure. Progressions and modulations of structural elements in one sequence as well as the entirety of series resemble due to visual rhythm and timing, written or even spoken language.
However, each individual artwork of the ZERO artists does not claim to mean anything by itself. They do not attempt to symbolize anything or try to provide content. These artworks consist of sequences of structural elements; each individual unit is not filled with intrinsic meaning, and is therefore individually of no structural significance. It is the totality of these elements, which constitutes a new perception of structure.
Consequently, no semantic motion is present, which, for this reason, was excluded from the outset of the analysis. The missing semantic meaning of

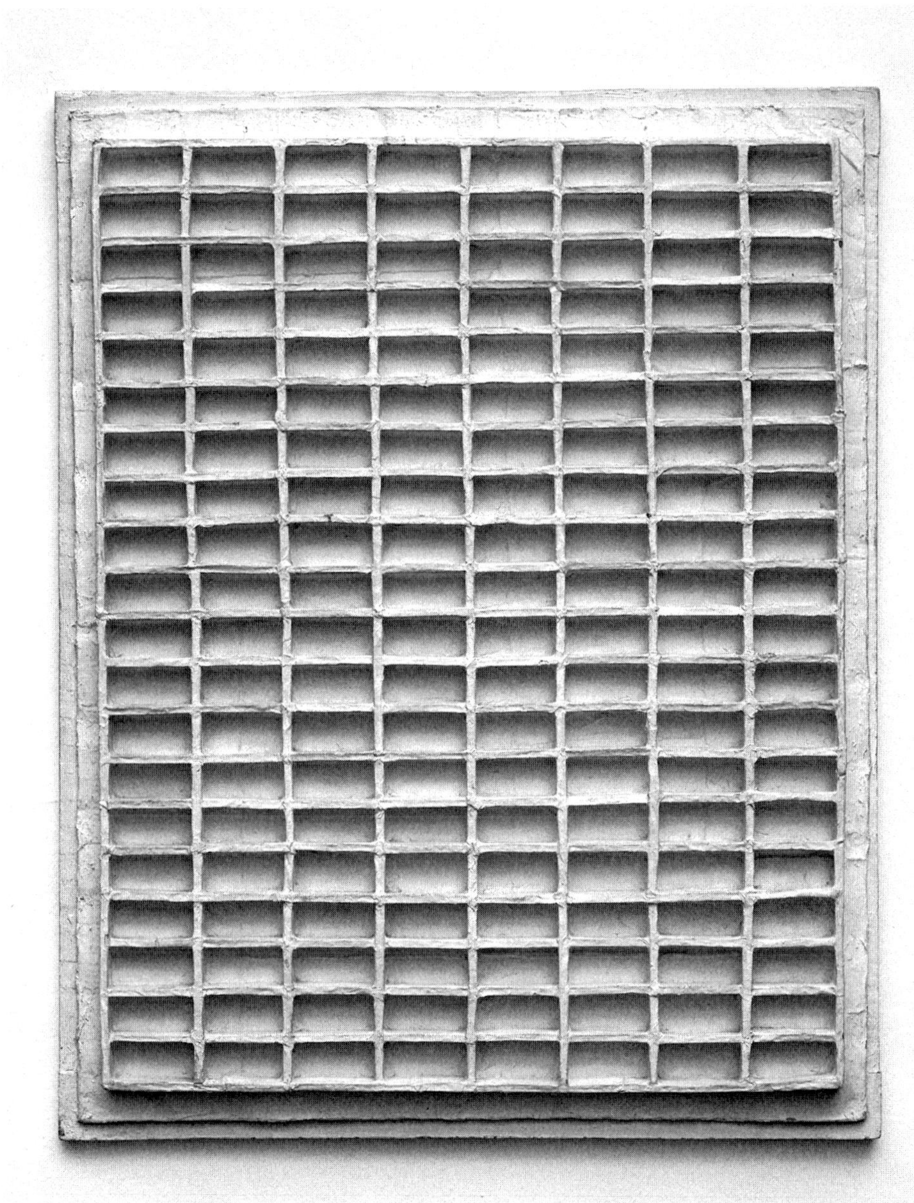

Fig. 6. Jan Schoonhoven, *Weißes Strukturrelief R 62-1*, 1962, 100 x 60 cm, painted papier maché on wood. Formerly Collection Lenz Schönberg, Söll/Tirol, present owner unknown. © VG Bild-Kunst, Bonn 2014. Photo: Philipp Schönborn, München.

signs challenges the observer. The artwork is approached with individual experiences, knowledge and associations while reading its structures. This process creates a subjective matter only based on structure. According to Umberto Eco, the Italian semiotician and literary critic, and his theory of the "open work", the beholder's presence and his contemplation completes the artwork and fills it, as it were, with individual content.[32] Therefore, each reading might differ from another. This offers manifold interpretations to one piece of structural art. Using language within a linguistic community, on the other hand, is based on conventions and therefore fixed meanings behind each linguistic unit.

The substitutions that help to translate a system of signs into the language of another system – according to the initial quote by Lévi-Strauss – might be seen in the aesthetic implementation. Instead of words, structure creates the basis for an aesthetic and phenomenological experience that forces its observers to contemplation and cognition.

In emblems, the beholder is confronted with a syntactical trisection, namely a *motto*, an image or *pictura* and a *subscriptio*. Based on the given headline, the short textual explanation and the picture, the reader of the duality of image and text has to decode the given structure in order to perceive the underlying message. Here, the picture as well as the text form a unity of meaning, which can only be understood if the reader or beholder shows a high degree of personal initiative or education. In this sense, visual structures and emblematic strategies operate similarly, as the missing semantic sign or content challenges the viewer.

Despite many differences between emblematic strategies and the presented field of research, a parallel can be drawn on a syntactic level; whereas emblematic strategies oppose text and picture in order to bring form and content into harmony and to understand its combining message, the intention of this research was not to analyze the connection between text and picture, but to analyze formal elements in both systems. Here, the analysis has primarily focused on the comparison of a limited selection of artists as well

32 Umberto Eco, *Das offene Kunstwerk*, Frankfurt am Main 1977 [first published in Italian 1962. For the English version see Umberto Eco, *The open work*, trans. Anna Cancogni, Cambridge, Mass. 1989].

as a specific section of linguistic studies. In terms of more complex serial arrangements, like Günther Uecker's nail structures resembling an illustrated melody comparable to (spoken) language, it appears worthwhile to broaden the scope of this research. Accordingly, the presented analysis makes a first contribution to a rarely investigated field of research and raises prospective issues.

The above analysis confirmed that linguistic structures are transferable to serial structures as in the artworks of the ZERO group, and consequently legitimates a comparison to both systems. It has been shown that serial structures are an integral element of the examples discussed. They have been compared to language structures to point out that with regard to the regular arrangement of signs or structural elements, it is possible to speak, on a syntactic level, of a translation of the system of language into art.

Diagrammatic Aspects in Contemporary Art

Maren Wienigk

Emblems are a unique and independent form of art, in which elements of texts and images are bound together in a specific order on a two-dimensional base material. The period of prosperity was between the 16th and 18th century. The classical structure of the printed emblem consists of a title at the top, an illustrating image in the middle part and an explanatory text below the image. The plenitude of artworks which produce combinations of images and texts is still immense in contemporary art as well as in the art historical positions of the 20th century. Less classical composed or structured, but highly polymorphic specifications of text-image-combinations can be found in the works of young contemporary artists. The spectrum of those works, which can be viewed and read, is huge. These works of text-image-combinations are characterized as notative, correspondent, concrete-poetical, binary, cartographic, biographic, archiving, speechless, opposing, formative, pellucid and also diagrammatical. Diagrammatic aspects additionally combine elements of image and texts with those of mathematical geometric components. Especially young artists use images and texts diagrammatically, i.e. in combination with mathematical geometric conventions. The goal of this essay is to show the possibilities of diagrammatic tools in contemporary art by reference to four selected works displayed in an exhibition of the Kunsthalle zu Kiel titled 'Nets: Weaving Webs in Art'.[1]

1 *Nets. Weaving Webs in Art*, exh. cat. Kunsthalle zu Kiel, ed. Anette Hüsch, Bielefeld 2014. The Kunsthistorische Institut of the Christian-Albrechts-Universität zu Kiel has been asking

Nets and Networks

The net became an essence and a point of culmination of research and thoughts for the exhibition in the Kunsthalle – on a metaphorical, historical and virtual level. A net consists of both lines or edges and dots or knots. It offers the possibility to trace very different ways of combinations. The naturally spun web of a spider, both filigree and extremely resistant, consists of threads that form the paths of the spider as well as glued threads that help to capture the prey. Combined, they form a complex structure. The web of a spider is its outsourced sensory system through which the environment is perceived: convulsions, new prey, air drafts, rain, and dew drops. The net functions equally as a trap and as a shelter. It oscillates between those meanings in mythological, biblical and historical contexts. During the 19th century, nets receive a lot of attention: the building of railways and the track systems, the electricity grids, telephone networks, and sewerage systems. Today, nets are ubiquitous. Putting it socially, nets and networks offer possibilities to question classical hierarchies. This is because nets and networks are more flexible and adjustable, as they enable to change and combine different elements. The most recent daily used and highly influential net is the Internet. It allows a global and immediate exchange of information.

Diagrams in Contemporary Theory

Diagrams can be described as nets represented on a plane base. Through graphical configuration such as lines, interleaves and topological disposal, they combine all given data with the goal to show the information and the resulting conclusions in a way which is vivid, comprehensible, and interpretable. Diagrams use and combine both images and texts. Images can be seen at once; they can be viewed immediately as well as examined for details.

the Kunsthalle zu Kiel to conceive an exhibition on the occasion of the Tenth International Conference of the Society of Emblem Studies. The exhibition shows the scope of natural and digital nets, during research we have been in touch with a lot of different aspects of image and texts unions.

Texts are linear and they require that the reader follows the consecutive lines in order to understand the content. Diagrams combine elements of images and texts in special relations and they demand the viewer to observe as well as to read. Diagrams make use of mathematical components such as proportions and coordinates. This observation has already been discussed by philosophers, philologists, culture scientist and art historians, who put diagrams into the focus of their research.[2] Until a few years ago, there was a peculiar imbalance between the frequent usage of diagrams in various contents and the outstanding theoretical thoughts of the function of diagrams: "the practical meaning of diagrams was not in proportion to the metalinguistic reflection". [3] Meanwhile, different approaches are distinguished encompassing the term, the genre, or the application.[4] The key features of diagrams are: constitution of meaning through generating sense on a plane surface by combining text-image-elements; visualization of relations by putting information into a special balance, and the pragmatical potential which can be used for additional actions. The scope of diagrams ranges from maps of paddocks, family trees and cosmologic overviews through geometric constructions, technical drawings, mechanical explanations, analytic diagrams of the proportions of the human body to maps, instructions, stock exchange price indices, metro maps, to name a few. All these examples combine given data with geometric conventions, distinctions, and dichotomies. This means that diagrams use graphic components, such as delimitations, blanks, and juxtapositions. They show the relations between the data and the results.

2 See especially: Steffen Bogen and Felix Thürlemann, "Jenseits der Opposition von Text und Bild. Überlegungen zu einer Theorie des Diagramms und des Diagrammatischen", in: *Die Bildwelt der Diagramme Joachims von Fiore. Zur Medialität religiös-politischer Programme im Mittelalter*, ed. Alexander Patschovsky, Ostfildern 2003, 1-22. – Frederik Stjernfelt, *An Investigation on the Borderlines of Phenomenology, Ontology, and Semiotics*, London 2007. – Sybille Krämer, "Operative Bildlichkeit. Von der 'Grammatologie' zu einer 'Diagrammatologie'? Reflexionen über erkennendes 'Sehen'", in: *Logik des Bildlichen. Zur Kritik der ikonischen Vernunft*, eds. Martina Hessler and Dieter Mersch, Bielefeld 2009, 94-123.

3 See Bogen/Thürlemann 2003 (as note 2), 8.

4 Sebastian Bucher, "Das Diagramm in den Bildwissenschaften. Begriffsanalytische, gattungstheoretische und anwendungsorientierte Ansätze in der diagrammtheoretischen Forschung", in: *Verwandte Bilder. Die Fragen der Bildwissenschaft*, eds. Ingeborg Reichle, Steffen Siegel and Achim Spelten, Berlin 2007, 113-129.

Independent from historical grown structures, diagrams have in common that one uses maps to orient oneself, and that one is able to trace his ancestral roots within a family tree. Furthermore, diagrams help to understand technical processes. The core features and the functional pragmatic aspects of these examples show an explicit reference to reality.
A diagram combines three categories: firstly, script and text as terms are used with explications supplemented with a legend, secondly, image and composition because they structure the diagram's meaning through the iconic elements in a simultaneously formed visual order, and thirdly, mathematics because it produces clearly defined relations.[5] Thus, the diagram comprehends its own form of thinking, demonstrating and representing. The linguist Christian Stetter defines diagrams as "graphic techniques for abbreviating complex schematizations," adding that "they preserve a minimum of the aesthetic quality that we need in order to understand what the discussion is about, and especially the things needed to literally visualize abstract content."[6] The diagram's balance between reality and abstraction can be observed in the London underground map created by the graphic designer

5 Felix Keller, "Ikonen der Moderne. Diagramme und die Ästhetik der Sichtbarkeit", in: *Das Wahre, Falsche, Schöne, Reality Show. Essays* (Lesen am Netz, vol. 1), eds. Walter Grond and Beat Matzenauer, Innsbruck 2005, S. 93-101.

6 See Christian Stetter, "Bild, Diagramm, Schrift", in: *Schrift. Kulturtechnik zwischen Auge, Hand und Maschine*, eds. Gernot Grube, Werner Kogge and Sybille Krämer, München 2005, 115-136, here 122 [translation by the author].

7 Sebastian Gießmann, "Henry Charles Beck. Material Culture and the London Tube Map of 1933", in: *Amodern* 2013, http://amodern.net/article/henry-c-beck-material-culture-and-the-london-tube-map-of-1933/ (accessed 20 October 2014).

8 See Stetter 2005 (as note 6), 122 and 125 [translation by the author].

9 See Stetter 2005 (as note 6), 123 [translation by the author].

10 Andreas Gormans, "Imaginationen des Unsichtbaren. Zur Gattungstheorie des Diagramms", in: *Erkenntnis, Erfindung, Konstruktion. Studien zur Bildgeschichte von Naturwissenschaften und Technik vom 16.–19. Jahrhundert*, ed. Hans Holländer, Berlin 2000, 51-72, here 53 [translation by the author].

11 Bogen/Thürlemann 2003 (as note 2), 5 [translation by the author].

12 See Bogen/Thürlemann 2003 (as note 2), 18 [translation by the author].

13 See Matthias Bauer and Christoph Ernst, ed., *Diagrammatik. Einführung in ein kultur- und medienwissenschaftliches Forschungsfeld* (Kultur- und Medientheorie), Bielefeld 2010, 12.

14 See Gormans 2000 (as note 10), 52.

15 Bauer/Ernst 2010 (as note 13), 10 [translation by the author].

16 See ill. in exh. cat. Kiel 2014 (as note 1), 140 and 141.

Henry C. Beck in 1931.[7] The routes of railways and the Thames are exclusively represented as horizontal, vertical or as forty-five-degree diagonal lines which differs from their actually course, yet is close enough to reality so that the viewer is able to find his position. According to Stetter, the diagram is "the exhibitive representation of a certain case with graphic instruments", and its function is a "schematized pictorial representation through a parametric system".[8] Following Stetter, a key feature of diagrams is "the classification of inscriptions as types", which highlights the notational characteristic of a symbol system in which every point of a diagram line can correlate to one segment of a parameter.[9] The art historian Andreas Gormans draws the conclusion that diagrams are pictures "which serve knowledge".[10] The basic features of diagrammatic structures are "the topological composition and the dichotomy structure of signs".[11] This means that both the actual coordinates of a point and its relation to other signs provide information. Diagrams illustrate structures of content on a level of binary relations by displaying analogies and contrasts through topological and typographical categories.[12] Diagrams consist of signs and blanks.[13] A diagram is formed by simple components such as lines, blanks and geometric fundamental forms. This simplicity of the two-dimensional structure seems inversely proportionate to the complexity of the explained phenomena.[14] Diagrams are joints between "cognition and imagination" and also between "sensuality and reason".[15]

Four Examples of Diagrammatic Artworks

The following passages introduce four works of art, in which the combination of pictorial, textual and geometrical elements is realized in different ways and with various techniques. All of them feature diagrammatic aspects. The Berlin philosopher and artist Marcus Steinweg understands diagrams as central tools for his artistic expression. His work *Philosophy as Art* (fig. 1) appears like a classic diagram.[16] It is a horizontally aligned large-scale collage, which combines written texts by Steinweg with the application of colored markers and tape. The used colors blue, black and red allow the distinction of the following categories: Steinweg's own thoughts are framed in blue, summaries are framed in black, and the names of philosophers are

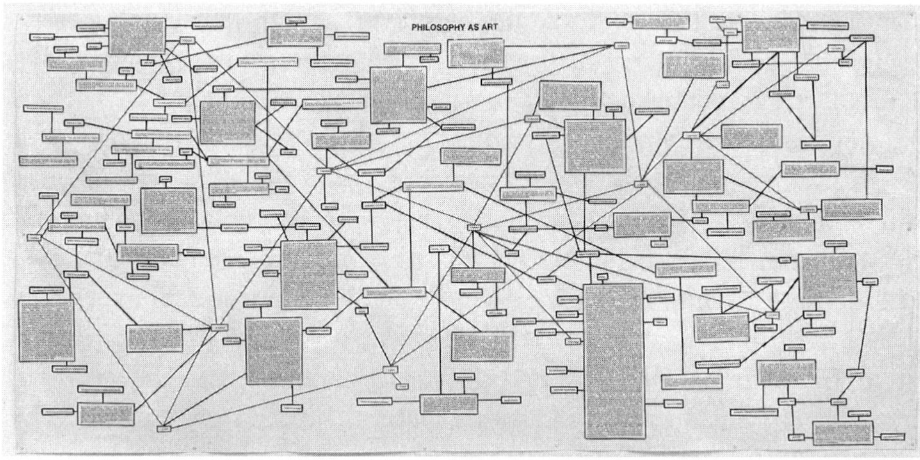

Fig. 1. Marcus Steinweg, *Philosophy As Art*, 2012, laser print, edding pen, tape on paper, 133 x 280 cm. © BQ, Berlin. Photo: Roman März, Berlin.

framed in red. Besides their framing function, the colors also serve to connect different philosophers and ideas. The conjunctive lines are structured in three ways: horizontally, vertically or diagonally. This formed net of lines plays with figure and ground on the given flat surface. It also plays with the oppositions of filled and empty spaces and with those contents which are situated in the middle of the sheet of paper and those toward the edges. It is possible to find a way into the diagram from all sides, either by observing, or reading the diagram. There are different ways of beginning with this reading process which differs considerably from reading a text that starts at the top left and ends at the bottom right corner of a page. The decisions one has to make determine the ways and effects of perception and knowledge. On the one hand, the graphical overview given in *Philosophy as Art* shows and structures the abundance of philosophical aesthetic arguments. On the other hand, due to the combined tools of graphic elements and printed text, the artwork might also seem cluttered giving no educational insight at all.
The Romanian artist Dan Perjovschi contributed his work *The July Report* (fig. 2) to the exhibition in Kiel.[17] The work fills the whole gallery of the

17 See examples of ill. in exh. cat. Kiel 2014 (as note 1), 159.

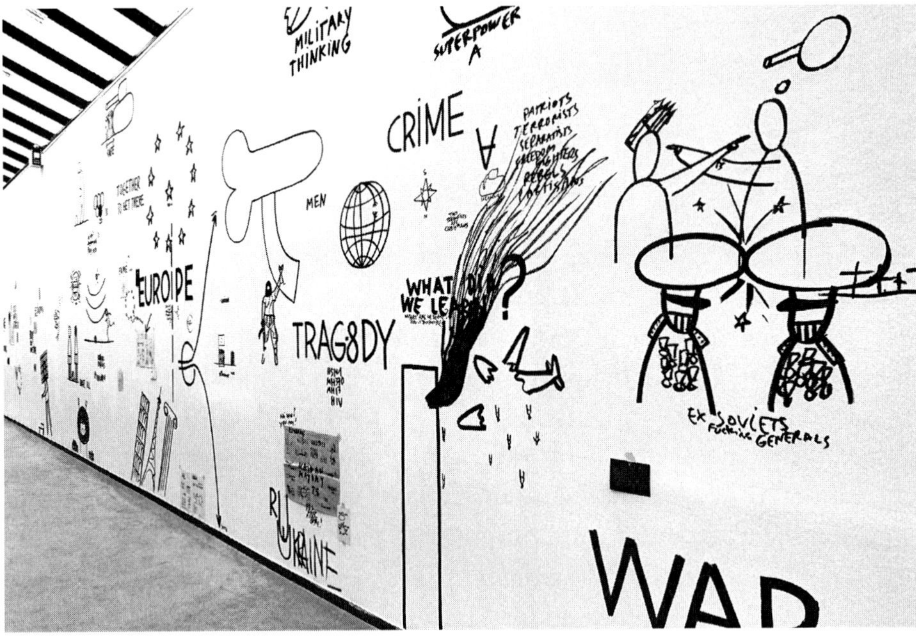

Fig. 2. Dan Perjovschi, *The July Report*, 2014, (detail), edding pen on wall, various dimensions, mural in the Kunsthalle zu Kiel. © Dan Perjovschi. Photo: Helmut Kunde.

Kunsthalle (approx. 30 x 3 meters). In his very own condensed pictural language, Perjovschi combines topics such as the football world cup 2014, the downing of a passenger plane over the Ukraine, the war in Gaza, capitalist chasms, racist remarks and institutional and financial mannerism of the art world – as well as personal impressions of working in Kiel. Perjovschi commented on the weather, the cruise liners and specific street names. He succeeds in the combination of a few strokes and words to hit the mark by visualizing an actual contemporary image of the international situation, and to interlink the variety of topics with each other. For *The July Report* in Kiel, Perjovschi additionally decided to combine his compact, concentrated and well emphasized drawings with postcards or illustrations he made for papers or magazines. This way he plays with the flatness of the wall and interlinks the contents on a further level by using contemporary and older drawings. Perjovschis method is straightforward and thereby genuinely contemporary: he draws directly on the walls, floors, windows, black boards and facades of different institutions. Those works are visible for just a certain period of time. The work *The July Report* discloses itself to the observer through walking by and combining all elements of texts, images and topics. At the same time, it is possible to start beholding and reading the work from various positions. *The July Report* often provokes a dialogical effect; visitors show each other different hints hidden in the work, which is structured with signs and chains of signs.

The Dutch artist William Engelen repeatedly translates daily rhythms such as the durations of sleep, work, leisure time and eating into musical rhythms. The piece *Verstrijken für Bratsche* was made during a working residence in Vienna in 2009. The Dutch word 'Verstrijken' can be translated as "passing time". Engelen has written a meticulous diary for 19 days; he put down when he slept, what he ate, what he worked with and how he organized his leisure time adding his moods, likes and dislikes. In the beginning, the diary was a preparatory work and not supposed to be part of the work's final realization. This concept would change later on. Engelen developed a musical score by using his 32 sheets of notations. Each hour of the day was clocked into eight seconds using own symbols of notations as well as musical notations developed in the 1950s and 1960s by pioneers such as John Cage.[18] The score encompasses twelve sheets and one legend. The different fields of sleeping, eating, working, and leisure time are marked in the colors blue, green, red and yellow. They show the repetitions and thus the rhythms. Interpreted by violinist Dimitrios Polisoides, the listener can follow and read it based on the score. The notations are organized in horizontal consecutive lines. The structures of signs vary to a great extent; they are curled, jagged, curved as well as combined or loose.[19] The key to these musical language codes can be found in the legend. While listening to the music, the notational signs become immaterial, and the sound of the signs is translated by Polisoides. The score of Engelen is readable in a linear way, while at the same time there is the possibility to see all sheets at once and to start drawing comparisons. The viewer is able to look at the diary and the score in order to find similarities and relations.

The German artist Jenny Michel combines fragments of images and texts in her collages.[20] In her oeuvre she localizes real and fictional spaces, historical and imaginary times, paradises and mega cities and thereby creates an oscillation between philosophy, science and art. Technical drawings, circuit

diagrams and instructions are the base materials in three collages of the series *Anleitung zum Zumüllen des Paradieses*. Layers of translucent paper from different times and of different kind concentrate on a mechanic-poetical and fictional-fantastic mesh work. In these collages different materials such as semitransparent papers and plastic foils overlap with each other. The sheet *Ein Palimpsest-Gehirn hängt über der Maschinenlandschaft*, based on a technical paper from older times, shows two areas: In the lower part, graphical black and white elements of images circle between technical plans and filigree play, and form a surreal landscape. In the upper part, yellowed and typewritten paper-lines merge with translucent pieces of words, which creates the shape of a cloud similar to the graphical presentation of a brain.
Another work is titled *Das Paradies-Vehikel auf dem Weg ins Paradies/ Paradieshafen*. It shows a dysfunctional vehicle arriving at a connection point. Parts of the sheet blend into a unit of technical parts, technical signs and handwritten additions. It is reminiscent of Albrecht Dürer's *Triumphwagen* published in 1522. This vehicle is heading in the other direction and is accompanied by mythological female figures, which are combined with text passages typeset in 'Fraktur' font, which had been invented at that very time.
Jenny Michel's third collage displayed in the exhibition covers almost the whole surface of the base paper. Titled *Staubmaschine II mit Versatzstücken menschlicher Kultur zugemüllt*, it shows densely ordered, overlapping and interfering parts of writing which grow into a cross section of a technical machine. It is only possible to read small details and text fragments, while other parts of the work become unreadable due to dense overlays. Through the combining process these circuit diagrams, technical cross sections and mechanical details generate a more organic, rather than technical whole.

18 For the discussion of processes of notation see: *Notation. Kalkül und Form in den Künsten*, exh. cat. Akademie der Künste Berlin and ZKM Zentrum für Kunst und Medientechnologie Karlsruhe, ed. Hubertus von Amelunxen et al., Berlin 2008.

19 See ill. in exh. cat. Kiel 2014 (as note 1), 179.

20 See ill. in exh. cat. Kiel 2014 (as note 1), 164-165.

Diagrammatic Strategies in Contemporary Art

Each of the four examples follows a different strategy and uses its own materials. Producing a heterogeneous mixture of text-image-combinations in contemporary art, they are intended for being either viewed or read. Additionally, the viewer is asked to relate the given information of the different levels in order to combine and interpret the elements of images and texts. Thus, the process of viewing and reading is expanded in order of the specific form, structure, and direction. Here, one is able to identify a family resemblance between conceiving a diagram and conceiving an emblem: both are conceived through the double process of reading and viewing. Furthermore, they interlink all elements on the plain surface.

Engelen uses musical notations in a linear and strict order. The legend makes it possible to decode the scope and understand the notation as such. The whole piece *Verstrijken für Bratsche* contains the daily notations and the interpreted music. Steinweg, Michel und Perjovschi use the technique of the collage differently. The technique of collage is a tenor in modern artistic procedures that is characterized through collecting, choosing, opposing, through mounting, deconstructing, disintegrating, overlaying, and confronting with the help of cutting and tearing.[21] The peculiar potential of plainness and flatness is shown in the explicit juxtaposition of different elements in collages, which makes the coexistence in two-dimensional space the genuine signature of construction – in contrast, for example, to the depth-oriented perspective painting. The collage combines disparate material from different times and allows dense overlays, skippings, blanks, and tearings. As an artistic technique, it symbolizes also those processes of thinking based on parts of texts, slip boxes, snippets as well as on deletions and vacancies. In *Philosophy as Art,* Steinweg uses the technique of collage in a very strict and ordered way. In Michel's series *Anleitung zum Zumüllen des Paradiese* the collage technique is used in a overlaying, organic and condensed manner. *The July Report* by Perjovschi combines older illustrations with the newly created illustrations inside the museum. As in a collage,

[21] See Franz Mon, "Arbeitsthesen zur Tagung 'Prinzip Collage'", in: *Prinzip Collage,* ed. Institut für moderne Kunst Nürnberg, Neuwied et al. 1968.

diagrams use the possibilities of arrangements and operations on a two-dimensional surface: one line already divides it into two parts. In all cases there will be an upper and a lower part, a left and a right part. Especially the arrangement and, in addition, the combining of heterogeneous materials on a surface, establishes connections which show diagrammatic properties such as topological arrangements and dichotomist divisions. In spite of and because of their geometric conventions, diagrams are able to evoke astonishing and surprising effects and puzzles. The technical paper providing the base of Michel's collages gives an idea of rationality and predictability. This impression reverses itself when faced with the numerous unreadable parts of words. In its composition, Steinweg's *Philosophy as Art* suggests through its complex organizing and with its confusing lines that the process of thinking cannot come to an end. Also, it is impossible to represent it in one graphic as it emerges and evolves in repetitive reading combined with questions. In this graphic overview, the reading viewer will find new approaches and questions time and again.

All of these art works can be viewed and read in a non-linear way – they even ask for it or force it. From just two dimensions they unfold compressed spaces, in which complex processes of reception take place. The potentials of diagrammatic compositions in contemporary art are displayed by means of the openness of origin, direction, way and completion combined with the detachment of conventions in representational techniques as well as processes of notation. There are a several possibilities of reading a diagram and finding a direction comparable to the processes of viewing and reading an emblem. Also, another parallel can be drawn in processes of agglomeration, coding and decoding.

Schriften aus dem Kunsthistorischen Institut der Christian-Albrechts-Universität zu Kiel

hrsg. von Prof. Dr. Klaus Gereon Beuckers, Prof. Dr. Christoph Jobst und Prof. Dr. Uwe Albrecht

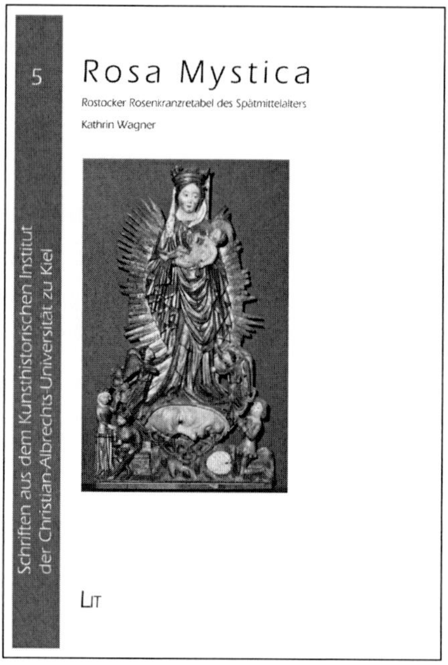

Kathrin Wagner
Rosa Mystica
Rostocker Rosenkranzretabel des Spätmittelalters

Die Mal- und Schnitzwerkstätten der Hansestadt Rostock florierten besonders im 15. Jahrhundert. In ihnen wurden nicht nur die Hochaltarretabel der städtischen Pfarr- und Ordenskirchen hergestellt, sondern auch kleinere Retabel für die Nebenaltäre der Stadtkirchen und für Kirchen im mecklenburgischen und skandinavischen Raum. Es ist anzunehmen, dass der Typus des Rosenkranzretabels entwickelt wurde, um von der Kult- und Wallfahrtstradition um eine Pietà in der Rostocker Marienkirche zu profitieren. Der vorliegende Band gilt als Ergänzung zu dem 2011 erschienenen Buch *Rostocker Retabelkunst im 15. Jahrhundert.*

Bd. 5, 2014, 64 S., 24,90 €, br., ISBN 978-3-643-12381-7

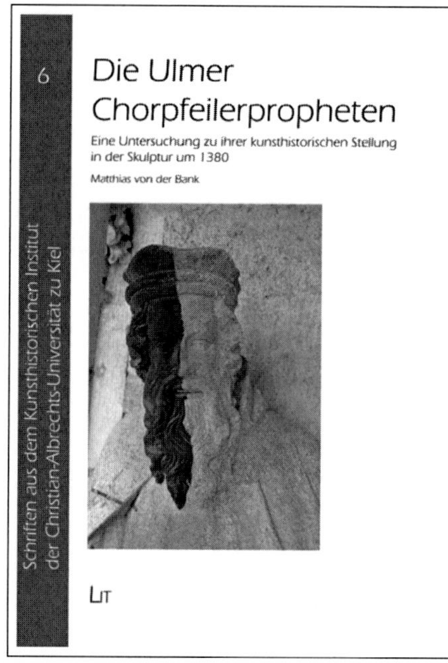

Matthias von der Bank
Die Ulmer Chorpfeilerpropheten
Eine Untersuchung zu ihrer kunsthistorischen Stellung in der Skulptur um 1380

Die Ulmer Chorpfeilerpropheten gehören zu den herausragenden Skulpturen aus der Zeit um 1380. Dennoch fanden sie in der Kunstgeschichte bisher nur wenig Beachtung, weil sie unzugänglich hoch oben am Ulmer Münsterchor stehen. Erstmals ist eine wissenschaftliche Untersuchung dieses bedeutenden Ensembles aus unmittelbarer Nähe durch die Restaurierung des Chores möglich geworden. Die Ergebnisse der kunsthistorischen Analyse der einzelnen Propheten im Kontext der parlerischen Skulptur wird mit diesem Band vorgelegt.

Bd. 6, 2014, 320 S., 34,90 €, br., ISBN 978-3-643-12833-1

LIT Verlag Berlin – Münster – Wien – Zürich – London

Auslieferung Deutschland / Österreich / Schweiz: siehe Impressumsseite